TYLER TRENT

with John Driver

Foreword by Scott Van Pelt, ESPN anchor

THE UPSET

LIFE (SPORTS), DEATH...AND THE LEGACY WE LEAVE IN THE MIDDLE

The Tyler Trent Story

The Upset
Life (Sports), Death . . . and the Legacy We Leave in the Middle
www.tylertrentbook.com

Copyright © 2019 by Tyler Trent

Published by The Core Media Group, Inc.,
P.O. Box 2037, Indian Trail, NC 28079
www.thecoremediagroup.com

Published in association with the literary agency of Wolgemuth & Associates.

Cover & Interior Design by Nadia Guy.
Photos in *The Upset* were provided by the Trent Family, ESPN, and Purdue
University.

ISBN 978-1-7323701-6-6

All rights reserved. No part of this publication may be reproduced, stored in
a retrieval system, or transmitted in any form or by any means — electronic,
mechanical, photocopy, recording, or any other — except for brief quotation in
printed reviews, without the prior written permission of the publisher.

Scripture quotations from The Holy Bible, English Standard Version® (ESV®), are
copyright © 2001 by Crossway, a publishing ministry of Good News Publishers.
Used by permission. All rights reserved.

Scripture quotations marked (NIV) are taken from the Holy Bible, New
International Version®, NIV®. Copyright © 1973, 1978, 1984, 2011 by Biblica,
Inc.™ Used by permission of Zondervan. All rights reserved worldwide. www.
zondervan.com The "NIV" and "New International Version" are trademarks
registered in the United States Patent and Trademark Office by Biblica, Inc.™

Scripture taken from the New King James Version is copyright © 1982 by
Thomas Nelson, Inc. Used by permission. All rights reserved.

Published in the United States of America.

Praise for *The Upset*

"*The Upset* is a touching reminder of the impact one person can have on the world. Tyler Trent blessed the country with his inspiring outlook on life and never let cancer overcome his love for his family, strong faith in God, and passion for Purdue football. He raised awareness for pediatric cancer research and the impact this disease has on families during his short time on Earth, and it is a true testament to his character that he continues to help those with cancer even after his passing. By reading this powerful and moving story about Tyler's journey, you, too, will join his fight against cancer. *#TylerStrong*."

Congresswoman Susan W. Brooks
Indiana's 5th Congressional District

"*The Upset* is a must-read primer for anyone touched by the great equalizer of cancer. Tyler humbly celebrated the gift of life in the midst of his battle, creating a sense of hope and calmness throughout his journey. His emotions were raw with reality and guided by purpose. In the rare instances when such a person comes along in our lives, however brief, we should all stop and reach for the unknown, the impossible, and that glimmering light in the dark. Read this book and learn from one of the most inspirational and motivating sports movements in history."

Gina Lehe
Senior Director of External Relations and Branding
College Football Playoff

"Tyler Trent's intelligence, heart, courage, and vision touched thousands of lives, and *The Upset* tells his remarkable tale. Tyler is an unforgettable young man with a powerful and poignant story. He changed my life. He'll change yours, too."

Adrian Wojnarowski
ESPN NBA Insider and *New York Times* Best-Selling Author

"Tyler Trent continues to be an extraordinary inspiration! I am truly thankful and blessed to have spent time with him and to personally experience his never-give-up attitude. Tyler's longtime devotion to Purdue football certainly earned him the title of Superfan, but there is much more to Tyler and much more to his story than that. Advocating and championing for cancer awareness and cancer research, Tyler motivated others to get involved in the fight to defeat cancer. He did something about his circumstances, and he battled with exceptional courage. His incredible gratitude, spirit, and tireless advocacy lifted others and made this world a much better place. Love you, Tyler!"

Chuck Pagano
Defensive Coordinator, Chicago Bears

"Some books are written, but some are *lived*. This is a book about the inspirational life of Tyler Trent. There is a saying that it's not the years in a life but rather the life in the years. I was truly inspired by the life of Tyler Trent and the way he lived it. God used a young man to inspire a community, a sport, and a nation. Tyler is truly an example of how to live and appreciate life. My life is better because of the spirit and courage that I saw in Tyler Trent. Through the pages of this book, yours will be, too. Thank you, Tyler, for impacting millions of lives through your challenge. May you rest in peace."

Coach Dabo Swinney
Head Football Coach, Clemson University

"Tyler Trent taught us how to truly live, how to walk boldly in our faith, how to love God wholeheartedly, how to trust God in all circumstances, and how to never, ever give up. Tyler told his story, and my hope is this: that we will all take the time to listen."

Matt Overton
NFL Long Snapper, Jacksonville Jaguars

"Tyler Trent was grit personified. Dealt a hand worse than any of us, he never stopped working, or fighting, or moving ahead. His courage, and faith, and even cheerfulness amid such bad luck set an example none of us could miss and all of us will be better for witnessing firsthand. Years from now, we'll all be telling people, 'I was at Purdue with Tyler Trent.'"

Mitch Daniels
President, Purdue University

"Tyler's book is a poignant and honest discussion of his emotional path to death and how his faith sustained him. Tyler viewed his cancer as a blessing from God—His plan for Tyler to leave a legacy of a joyful and unyielding commitment to cancer research that he believed would help others. This is a must-read book for understanding how a young man—known only to a small circle of friends in Carmel, Indiana—ultimately reached a nation to tell them about God and the need to help through supporting cancer research."

Timothy L. Ratliff, PhD
Robert Wallace Miller Director
Purdue University Center for Cancer Research

"Tyler Trent bravely used his foundation of faith, love, and family to be a light in our world, seen and felt by so many. I imagine God is smiling about the impact Tyler made on this earth. His book will illuminate who Tyler was and why it mattered. My life will be forever blessed by being a friend of Tyler."

Tim Bobillo
Chief Development Officer
Purdue University Center for Cancer Research

"Tyler, through the way he lived his life and the message he shared, inspired not only the Purdue community, but an entire nation as well. This book is a must-read about an exceptional young man."

Jeff Brohm
Head Football Coach, Purdue University

"Even though his life was short, Tyler's legacy will live on forever. I cried when I heard Tyler passed away, but they were not tears of sadness; they were tears of hope. Hope that the world will learn that everyone has a story, and if we just take time to listen to them, we will have the same compassion and empathy for others that Tyler did. Hope that we take every opportunity to live life to the fullest, no matter how hard the circumstances we face. *The Upset* is a must-read for those who want to change the world and leave a legacy much like Tyler Trent."

Chris Ballard
General Manager, Indianapolis Colts
Indiana Farm Bureau Football Center

"Without ever putting on a helmet, or making a tackle, or scoring a touchdown, Tyler Trent became an essential figure in college football. But his story reaches so far beyond any sport. Through his testimony of faith, his courage to fight, and his desire to change the course of pediatric cancer, he touched a nation's soul and captured its heart. We sometimes confuse record with legacy. This is not only the record of a young man's life; it's the chronicle of a legacy—one that has power to resonate across so many seasons to come."

Tom Rinaldi
ESPN Correspondent

"Entering Tyler Trent's orbit wasn't hard, and this book will show you why. *The Upset* provides the behind-the-scenes story of the Jesus-centered faith, winsome candor, and inspiring strength of Tyler and his entire family. As Tyler's pastor, I've watched this amazing and painful journey unfold. Grab a tissue, and get ready to be changed. I can't wait for you to be moved to follow Jesus by what you're about to read in this incredible book."

Mark Vroegop
Lead Pastor, College Park Church, Indianapolis
Author of *Dark Clouds, Deep Mercy—Discovering the Grace of Lament*

"Few individuals have risen up and touched the heart of our nation like Tyler Trent. Tyler's unwavering faith in Christ and his determination to live life to its fullest empowered him to lead in the fight against pediatric cancer with the Riley Hospital for Children, all while carrying the mantle as Purdue's biggest fan. Through the life he lived, through the faith he shared, and now through the pages of this book, Tyler inspires us still, bringing fresh hope to countless others battling cancer and showing us all what it means to live a life of courage and consequence—to be Tyler Strong."

Michael R. Pence
Vice President of the United States

"Tyler Trent's journey is more than an inspirational story about a courageous, honest, and thoughtful young man battling difficult odds with bone cancer. His story is deeply transformational, as we allow ourselves to enter into the bigger story—God's story in Jesus Christ—that Tyler and the Trent family live inside of, and that each of us is invited into as well. As we enter in, we will understand how Tyler became *TylerStrong*!"

Newt Crenshaw
President and CEO, Young Life
Cancer Survivor

"*The Upset* is enticing. It reveals the personal life of superfan Tyler Trent before, during, and after his stunning encounter with the national spotlight. You'll experience a surprise victory over cancer and its unexpected result. And you'll walk away with a surprise encounter with God—the one ultimately responsible for Tyler's death *and* his legacy left on Earth. You'll encounter the faith of a man who comes face to face with his mortality and makes peace with his Creator. *The Upset* invites the reader to not only know the story of Tyler's fame, but to know Tyler—the college kid behind the legend. In classic Tyler fashion, this story will impact your life. You'll be challenged to think differently about your own life as you encounter the unpredictable story of his."

Joe Wittmer
Pastor of Local Outreach, College Park Church

"Tyler was an inspiration to all of us, whether we are in sports or not. In this book, Tyler shares a number of stories that help the reader tap into his personal struggles, triumphs, and amazing memories. It is clear that Tyler's mission in life was much more than his own battle with cancer. His words will continue to encourage people all around the world and will have a positive impact on countless lives."

Kevin Pritchard
President of Basketball Operations, Indiana Pacers

"I was grateful to have interviewed Tyler Trent, and I came away so impressed with the way he lived his life—with purpose, with hope, and with joy. His story impacted me greatly, and I think about him every day. I know it will impact you, too."

Jason Romano
Host, *Sports Spectrum Podcast*
Author of *Live to Forgive*

"Tyler Trent was an admirable young man. Despite facing his own battle with cancer, he became a voice and advocate for cancer research. I believe through his perseverance and selfless acts, we will find a cure. Tyler, you are a true champion."

Adam Vinatieri
NFL Placekicker, Indianapolis Colts

"How does Tyler Trent go from being an average college student standing in line for Purdue football tickets to one of our nation's most inspiring and most unforgettable people? Courage in the face of heartbreaking illness, a humbleness of character that he openly shared, and an unwavering faith in that something better awaits are all part of the answer. This book gives you a look at how and why Tyler was able to stand so strong and share his strength and faith. I have never met a person so strong, so devoted to his faith, and so unafraid of the inevitable. I hope reading his book inspires all to stay strong and stay faithful in the face of whatever life throws their way in the upset of life."

Dan Dakich
Host, the *Dan Dakich Show* on ESPN Radio
ESPN Basketball Analyst
Tyler's Friend

"Tyler Trent was as uplifting a human being as I've ever come across. His positivity in the face of adversity was beyond words, and the way that he rallied our Purdue community truly was amazing. I'm honored that I got to know such an inspiring young man and will forever heed his words."

Ryan Kerrigan
NFL Linebacker, Washington Redskins

"In Tyler Trent's *The Upset*, you will read the story of a remarkable young man; a story that is both heartbreaking and incredibly uplifting. While he was called from this earth at just twenty, his eternal perspective is what will resonate with you. Tyler always realized that no matter what life threw at him, his faith in Jesus Christ ensured that there was ultimately a glorious reward awaiting him. This book, like Tyler's life, is simply heaven-sent."

Ernie Johnson, Jr.
Sportscaster, TNT (Turner Network Television)
Author of *Unscripted—The Unpredictable Moments That Make Life Extraordinary*

"A *hero* is a person who is admired or idealized for courage, outstanding achievements, or noble qualities. Tyler Trent qualifies! Through the course of his journey, he bravely faced adversity, did not shrink back from physically daunting circumstances, and attained seemingly impossible goals. He did it all with a humility and authenticity that inspired those around him to be better people. *The Upset* candidly and genuinely gives us a closer look into his struggles, and perhaps most importantly, how he relied on his faith in Jesus Christ to become a true hero to us all."

Mark Ferrara
Senior Consultant
Talent Solutions, The Walt Disney Company

"Tyler Trent belongs on the Mt. Rushmore of inspirational cancer-fighting sports figures, alongside Jim Valvano and Stuart Scott. He amazed and inspired us by fighting cancer and living life on his terms. *The Upset* is an amazing story, and here it is in Tyler's own words."

Gregg Doyel
Sports Columnist, *The Indianapolis Star*

"Inspiring, captivating, and an example of true courage. Getting to be a member of Tyler Trent's story was life changing. Even if you've heard the story, you need to dive in and see how *The Upset* will give you an in-depth look at the joy, suffering, and impact of the most powerful story of 2019."

David Blough
Quarterback, Purdue University Football

"Inspirational, selfless, God-fearing, and flat-out *tough* are a few of the many words to describe Tyler. He galvanized many through his unwavering faith. He used his platform as a classroom to teach others how to approach life with an abundance of gratitude. He battled consistently, never complaining about his struggles, but instead helping us deal with our own. Tyler brought fight and grit to the one playing field we all have in common: *life*. Tyler had many titles—great son, brother, friend, student, etc.,—but through his journey, he gained another: *hero*."

Ja'Whaun Bentley
NFL Linebacker, New England Patriots
Super Bowl LIII Champion
Former Purdue Boilermakers Football Linebacker

"Tyler represented exactly what the Webster Dictionary defines as *courage*. His inspirational story captivated the nation, and he certainly became a hero to many who witnessed his courageous battle against osteosarcoma. Tyler passed on January 1, 2019. He may be gone, but he will never, ever be forgotten."

Dick Vitale
ESPN Analyst

"Tyler possessed a rare, God-given quality to allow adversity and suffering to *increase* his faith and dependence on God. As he faced wave after wave of challenges, I was privileged to watch him grow stronger as he went. He exuded joy and peace in the midst of his suffering that could only be explained by his trust in the God of hope. Undoubtedly, he will receive that crown promised to those who overcome and finish! May God use this book as he used Tyler's life to inspire others beyond what he might have asked or imagined."

Coach Clyde Christensen
Assistant Coach, Tampa Bay Buccaneers

"I never dreamed that taking a handful of Purdue football student-athletes to deliver a game ball to their classmate would have such an impact on me, but that visit, and Tyler's story, truly strengthened my view of what we should all strive to be. His daily message reinforced my lifelong tenets to serve others without reservation and to know that the bigger picture is always more immense than any one person. To say the least, he lived his life on his own terms, and that lesson should impact us all on a daily basis. To note that he is my hero does not even begin to describe what he, and his family, mean to me. I'll be eternally grateful to Tyler, Tony, Kelly, Blake, and Ethan for allowing me to be a part of their lives."

Matt Rector
Associate Strategic Communications Director
Purdue University Football

"Tyler's spirit and commitment to making life better for others dealing with similar circumstances while waging his own personal battle continue to be an inspiration to us all. That inspiration is why we salute Tyler as the recipient of the Disney Spirit Award."

Faron D. Kelley
Vice President
ESPN *Wide World of Sports*, *runDisney*,
and Disney's Water Parks

"Tyler taught a team what is possible when individuals play for something greater than themselves. He taught a university what is possible when you live for someone else. He taught a nation about the God who loved and sustained him every step of his journey. I hope I never forget all I learned from this exceptional young man. This story needs to be told."

Dave Tiley
Businessman
Purdue Alumnus

"In 2014, Tyler Trent was diagnosed with osteosarcoma, his first of three battles with cancer. What followed was a series of life decisions that led to a legacy that, even in death, was undefeated. Tyler knew that if he could make anything, he should make a difference. He made a difference in my life, and this book will make a difference in yours."

Trey Mock
Indianapolis Colts Mascot

"Tyler Trent's story is a powerful, heartfelt journey of courage and inspiration. In this book, Tyler shows us what we are all capable of in the face of adversity and how we should strive to live our lives."

Pete Ward
Chief Operating Officer, Indianapolis Colts
Indiana Farm Bureau Football Center

"Unfortunately, I never had the opportunity to meet Tyler, but I certainly heard his message, as did the entire college football world. I believe the impact of Tyler's life was, and will continue to be, so powerful because God empowered him to show everyone with eyes to see what a genuine life of gratitude looks like."

Todd Blackledge
ESPN College Football Analyst

"I am blessed to have crossed paths with Tyler Trent; but we met in the most unfortunate circumstances. I am a pediatric oncologist at Indiana University School of Medicine and the Director of the Precision Genomics Program at Riley Hospital for Children. I met Tyler when he developed relapsed osteosarcoma in May 2017. It was a day that forever changed Tyler and his family with the tragedy of having relapsed, aggressive cancer. Yet, without this horrible event, I may never have met this incredibly grounded, humble, and impactful young adult. I have always felt that getting to walk the path of pediatric cancer with each patient and family who we care for is one of the greatest privileges of my life. However, there was something extraordinarily special about Tyler Trent. Cancer afflicts hundreds of thousands of people, including more than 15,000 children in the

U.S. every year; but it is almost unheard of for a teen with cancer to touch as many people as Tyler Trent did and continues to do. Why? How? What was so special about Tyler? Tyler's life was derailed by his relapsed cancer. He experienced sadness and anger just as anyone else does; but he refused to let cancer destroy him. Tyler experienced having to give up his hopes and dreams for his life; but he was so grounded in an incredibly strong faith that he was able to accept and actually embrace the fact that he was faced with embarking on a different path than he had planned. Tyler accepted his new mission for a life focused on sharing a message of hope and resilience. Even in the midst of doing everything he could to fight for his life, he kept on living life to the fullest and making the most of every single day. Tyler shared a message of hope for the future through more support for pediatric cancer research. While he knew this message was unlikely to help him personally, his dream was for his legacy to save the lives of kids in the future. He also was the quintessential living example of what it means to live a life that is meant for you. *The Upset* is an incredible story of Tyler's journey and the amazing legacy of hope that he has left behind."

Jamie L. Renbarger, MD, MS

"Tyler was such a special young man who provided so many people inspiration for the way he lived his life, especially during his valiant battle against cancer. His legacy and spirit will live forever!"

Kirk Herbstreit
ESPN Correspondent, College Football Analyst

"I, along with thousands of others across our nation, especially central Indiana, have been deeply impacted by Tyler's story—even more so by his insights, attitude, and perspective. He writes with the maturity of someone three times his age and with a spiritual depth that few achieve in a lifetime of following Jesus. His words in this book are real, honest, challenging, and encouraging. His humor and humility combine to draw us into a conversation that none of us want to have, but must. He relentlessly keeps bringing us back to the hope that he held onto so tightly. Do you have questions about the difficulties and unfair trials of life? Let Tyler walk you through some of those. Let him loan you some of his courage and strength. May it lead you to the same hope that he knew."

Aaron Brockett
Lead Pastor, Traders Point Christian Church, Indianapolis

Contents

Foreword

by Scott Van Pelt, ESPN SportsCenter Anchor, Golf Host

My grandmother, Letha Casazza, was the greatest testimony to faith—and the greatest woman—I've ever known. She spent her entire life in service to others. She didn't believe in God; she *knew* her God.

I used to love to stay at her house for "slumber parties." The highlight was when she'd lie down with me as I fell asleep. We'd talk about anything and everything. Inevitably, the conversation would turn to God. I vividly recall once asking her about heaven and how she knew it was real. As I write this, I can see her beautiful face, bathed in the light from the hallway as she smiled and told me, "I just know."

What do you *hope*? What do you *believe*? What do you *know*?

I *hope* that Tyler Trent's story inspires you, me, and everyone to fight the disease that took his life.

I *believe* that his story will lead to millions of dollars in donations to fight cancer.

I *know* I didn't meet him by accident.

When Pastor Mark Vroegop spoke at Tyler's celebration on January 8, 2019, in the College Park Church in suburban Indianapolis, he could have been speaking to any of the thousands in that beautiful room. But I know he was speaking to me.

I *know* it.

"If your life intersected with Tyler's, it wasn't an accident." When I spoke with Mark afterward, I wasn't quite able to get through it without crying. I just wanted to thank him for saying what I already knew.

Tyler and I came into one another's orbit for a reason: so that I might amplify the story of the fight of this young warrior. We met because he was a sports writer and fan, and because my friend and coworker Adrian Wojnarowski had his number. Woj has *everyone's* number. He shared it with me, and I texted Tyler just to let him know I was out there and that I was praying for him. It could have ended with a couple of texts.

But it didn't.

After Purdue's upset of Ohio State, we texted back and forth, and he told me, "Let me know if you ever need anything. It would fulfill a dream of mine to work with you!"

Without hesitation, my reply was, "So, let's work together." That was on Monday, October 22. On Wednesday, October 24, Tyler was my "cohost," and we taped a segment for that night's show.

For the nearly twenty years I have been at ESPN, I've been fortunate to cross paths with basically every big-time coach and player out there. They don't make me nervous. My dad taught me a simple lesson: treat superstars like normal people, and treat normal people like superstars.

I was prepared to treat Tyler like the superstar he was, but I was scared. I didn't know if he was up to it. He was in hospice care. He was dying, right? What if this was a mistake? I didn't want to do anything that would be a detriment to his care. So I called his father, Tony, to make sure this was okay. He reassured me that this was what Tyler wanted to do.

When I walked into our studio that night, I saw Tyler on a giant screen on a wall. His eyes were bright and alive. A smile spread across his face. In an instant, I was at ease. I had prayed all day, hoping for strength to get through this. The Lord delivered that strength through the twenty-year-old on the other end of the camera whose body was riddled with cancer.

How on Earth was Tyler the stronger one of the two of us? As he will tell you, it's quite simple: God. Tyler's unshakable faith in Jesus Christ was the source of his strength in the face of a fight that could have extinguished it. His hope in sharing his story and his faith is that they might strengthen yours. He also hopes that his story can be a catalyst in ending cancer. Our paths crossed so that I could help him share that story.

As everyone knows, this was a passionate Purdue fan. I often have thought about their cartoonish mascot, Pete, and the hammer he wields. Tyler closed his segment with me with their battle cry: "Boiler up . . . hammer down."

I feel like Tyler is the one with the hammer now. He was armed with faith, and the strength of that faith is behind him, still swinging that hammer . . . to obliterate cancer from beyond the grave with a story that will outlive us all.

It's a story of *hope*, *belief*, and *knowing* where he was headed when the end came.

You have this book in your hands for a reason. You might not know what the reason is yet, but you will.

It's not an accident.

I *know* it.

Collaborative Writer's Note

by John Driver

My name is John Driver . . . and this is the only moment in this book you will hear *my* voice. I like it this way. After all, you are about to hear from one of the most remarkable people I've ever had the honor of knowing.

My prediction is that you will find him remarkable as well.

So even though I would rather just get to the good stuff found in Tyler's story, there are a few things I think you should know first. Taking a few minutes of your time right here at the beginning gives me a chance to share insights about Tyler and his family that they will never tell you. They are way too humble to do that. Thus, I would be remiss if I did not offer a couple of observations about the details of our writing process and the context of the story in the pages ahead.

This Moment Truly Is No Accident . . . and Here's Why

If this book is about anything, it's that you're not here by accident. Scott Van Pelt has already beautifully articulated this point in his foreword, regarding his own introduction to and interaction with Tyler. But even if you never actually met Tyler, I want you to know that it's also true about you and the book you now hold in your hands:

this is no accident.

When I first met Tyler Trent in the fall of 2018, his body was already completely paralyzed, except for his right arm. His normally razor-sharp mind, tucked inside his feeble body, was already beginning to experience momentary fogginess. There were lapses due to the devastating effects of the tumors living throughout his body, as well as the poisonous chemotherapy that had coursed through his veins hundreds of times over the previous four years. Trust me, he still had an amazing level of clarity and quick-wittedness, all things considered. But even so, you might wonder how a young man in his deteriorating condition could possibly have the time and energy to personally pen his own story in just a few months, his body melting away in a hospice bed.

This is a great question—and the answer unveils just a few of the diverse rays of colored light refracted from the divine prism of Tyler Trent's life and story. In fact, if I tell you how all this came together, I'm not sure you will even believe me—but I'll give it a try anyway.

First of all, Tyler was a brilliant writer in his own right, as you will come to discover. He had written many articles and spoken at numerous events. These writings and speeches helped lay the foundation for continuing his message through the writing of his story; before stepping into heaven, he had already said so much at such a young age.

I was honored to be able to begin writing this book by his side, both of us acutely aware that he might not be around to help us finish it. The process of collaboration is one most people are unfamiliar with, but let me tell you that Tyler was already a pro. His own feedback, edits, and clarity of vision and voice for the entire story and message this book contain reflect who he is to a "T" ("T" standing for Tyler, of course).

As you will learn, Tyler was the kind of guy who knew exactly what he wanted to say and how he wanted to say it, so we took measures early in the process to ensure that everything he wanted to say would be clearly heard, even if he wasn't able to polish every word himself. Second, the many stories written and broadcast about Tyler when his story became nationally prominent added another essential layer of information and authenticity to the writing of this story. Everyone who had any footage of Tyler seemed to be compelled to share it—with no credit requested and no strings attached. You don't have to work in the media industry to understand just how rare this truly is—and how thankful I am for their generosity.

The fact that Tyler had said so much in his short life is already atypical, but it is nothing less than a marvel that so much of it was captured on film. Specifically, ESPN went out of its way to graciously provide raw footage of interviews with Tyler and his family that the general public has never seen. They, along with every other contributor to our research, have truly honored Tyler's life and mission with their selfless willingness to help tell his story.

Next, Tyler entrusted the completion of this process to the people he loved the most—his parents and family. They were by his side throughout his life, so he knew it would be up to them to continue telling his story when he could no longer muster the strength to do so. Tony and Kelly Trent have worked tirelessly to honor Tyler's wish for this book to be written and published with accuracy and excellence. This they have done at great personal expense and risk, when necessary. And let's not forget that they have done this while caring for their beloved son in his last days, as well as the rest of their precious family. They are extraordinary parents, but even more than this, they are extraordinary people—as you will soon see.

Finally, in my opinion, the craziest reason this book is in your hands today is the seemingly random actions of a young man named Scott McCoulgin, a close friend to Tyler and the Trents. At an early point in Tyler's odyssey, Scott approached Tyler to tell him he felt strongly in his heart that he should begin capturing Tyler's personal thoughts, reflections, and random impressions as he walked through the daily events of facing cancer. The tangible result of Scott's loving and humble dedication to Tyler is more than a terabyte of candid, personal footage of Tyler speaking directly to the camera—and by extension, directly to you—during almost every stage of his story. Consequently, the transcribed word count from these videos would be enough to fill more than one hundred pages of a book with raw, unedited content. I'm so thankful to Scott McCoulgin.

I wholeheartedly echo Scott Van Pelt and add to his sentiments my belief that you are not reading these pages by accident.

This Is Tyler's Book, and He Asked for Our Help

Now that you better understand the astonishing alignment and timing of Tyler's story with its caretakers, each of these friends wants you to know that this book was a dream that Tyler desperately wanted to come true. In fact, Tyler mentioned this book in one of the last comments I found deeply embedded in one of the final personal interviews Tyler ever gave. He simply said that he needed to find a writer—a collaborator—to help him get started.

I can't adequately express to you how privileged I am to serve Tyler in this way.

So in terms of narrative tone, Tyler's is the predominant voice you will read. These are his thoughts and sentiments, mined and refined from all the sources and processes listed previously. He loved this book in its early stages and felt that it accurately reflected his words, voice, and message. He was an uncommonly intelligent person with a keen sense of wit and a profound awareness of his present life situation *as* he was actually living in it. Again, this is rare. It's just Tyler.

He also wanted the voices of his family and friends to be a part of this story. So, multiple chapters written by Tony and Kelly are scattered throughout the story. You will also hear from Tyler's two younger brothers, Blake and Ethan, as well as many of his other family members, friends, pastors, and national voices from sports and the media, in the epilogue. This book has been written in a way that appropriately reflects the way Tyler lived his life—with others, as a family and community affair.

You will also notice the unique treatment of the word "sports" in the book's subtitle. This is intentional—a creative reflection of the role sports played in Tyler's life and story. Sports is obviously not nearly as important as life and death, the very things Tyler faced day in and day out, but it was so significant to him nonetheless. Sports is the backdrop and context to so much of his story, whimsically nestled between the struggles and victories he faced as he fought against death, yet lived life to the fullest.

Thank you for affording me a few pages to frame this story and this process just a bit . . . I hope it helps you better understand how the book came to be. But now, I'll step aside. It's time for you to meet Tyler, the twenty-year-old man who has taught me so much about life (sports), death, and the legacy we leave in the middle.

CHAPTER 1

Unpredictable

(Tyler)

One of my favorite memories of childhood is the classic song "You Are My Sunshine." Every night, until I felt I had grown out of it, my mom would sing these lyrics to me as she tucked me into bed. Her sweet voice lifted my spirits. Every time. I didn't realize until sometime later how much these few, seemingly happy lines would impact me in such a lasting way.

In fact, after early childhood had passed me by, there were still times when I would become childlike again—scared, lonely, or upset. In those dark moments as I crawled into bed, I would quietly sing these familiar lyrics to myself. Mom's song had become my own. The song (the first three lines in particular) is filled with such joy as beautiful word pictures are painted about the happiness of love dissipating the cloudy skies of sadness—so much so that it's easy to somehow sing right past the tragic potential of pain tagged onto the end . . .

Please don't take my sunshine away.

Terminal Joy

When Mom sang to me, never in her wildest dreams—or even her most graphic nightmares—did she ever imagine that her "sunshine" might actually be taken away. But when I was fifteen years old, our family began living life in the last line of the song—in a place where a terminal illness threatened the very joy of life itself.

This overlooked line of the song hasn't just become ours; it has become the song of many families. Every single year, approximately 15,700 children are diagnosed with some form of cancer. For those parents, the last line of the song—their worst fear—is a reality. The "what ifs" come rushing into their minds in unyielding waves. After all, it is simply unnatural for children to die before their parents, let alone their grandparents. Children are supposed to be the future of a family. They are supposed to grow up. Learn to love. Learn to lose. And learn, just maybe, to even win a few. They are supposed to pursue their hopes and dreams.

To leave a legacy.

Over the course of the pages to come, alongside my family and friends, I share my hopes, dreams, and loves—and how cancer has attempted to obliterate these things. I also share a completely unpredictable turn of events that has brought unexpected strength into my life through my family, faith, and community. I also tell of the hope I have found in cancer research. Without family, faith, and community, I wouldn't be who I am today; but without cancer research, I quite literally would have been gone long before I had the first idea for this book.

There has been sunshine—faith and community have enriched my life in inexpressible ways. There has also been darkness—cancer research has only prolonged my life; it has not cured me. While I am thankful for the extra time, families like mine need more and more people to donate to cancer research every year. Without these investments, the careful study of this awful disease is not possible. This is why I am donating a portion of the proceeds from this book toward cancer research. My hope is that one day, a child with hopes and dreams just like mine may be able to live them out so that fewer families will have to reluctantly embrace the fear of having their sunshine taken away.

My hope is for all people in this world. For you. For all of us who face all the things that make us suffer from fear, including cancer or any of the other infinite difficulties of life. Whoever you may be, our family has joined your ranks. You are not alone. Together, we are the broken. We are the suffering.

Together, we are the upset.

I not only mean that we are a group of people feeling upset by our circumstances. You see, when we share these circumstances together, we can also become a different kind of upset—that unexpected convergence of unlikely variables in which an impossible win somehow emerges from seemingly utter hopelessness.

Hope truly exists for all of us—for you and for me. It is found in another kind of upset that is quietly brewing . . . one that beats the odds, ensuring our sunshine remains even if our lives are taken away.

Making Introductions

This is my story, which is actually difficult for me to say because the truth is, I don't really like it when all the attention is focused on me. You see, everyone has a story . . . the question is, will anyone ever hear it? I would rather talk about your story than my own—and that's the truth. But unfortunately, we don't have time for that because, well, my time is running out.

Am I *upset* about having terminal bone cancer at the age of twenty? Sure I am. As I write this, my entire body has surrendered to paralysis, except for my right arm, which I still use to journal on my iPad Pro, hold my iPhone to call my friends and family, and serve myself hot sips of Caramel Spice Lattes from the latest (daily, and sometimes more frequent) Starbucks run that my grandma has graciously made for me. I can't drink coffee anymore because they cause me migraines, but at least I still have my arsenal of Apple products and Starbucks.

But as far as my story goes, for now, you should know that this is my third matchup against osteosarcoma in the past five years. It has proven to be a formidable opponent, one that I hate with all the passion of a heated rivalry. I beat it the first time we faced each other, but apparently, there were more meetings on my schedule that I didn't see coming . . . and this time around, it's looking like the scoreboard is not in my favor.

This life—this book—these were definitely not my original ideas. This is not what I planned for my story. This was obviously not what my parents, friends, and family hoped for me, either. Yet here we are, living not the lives we dreamed about, but rather the lives we actually have right now.

What it really means to experience hope and life together—real, messy, difficult, hopeful, present life—is the primary focus, the ultimate goal of this book.

So to be clear, this is *not* a book about cancer. I refuse to give cancer such good publicity. No, my life—just like yours—is about so much more than just the accumulation of difficulties and impossibilities we face. We—you and me—have a life to live. Opponents to face. Odds to beat. Predictions to make. This is a book about a crazy story that has unfolded around me over the past five years—a story of family, real community, hope, and legacy.

As a sports statistician and sports writer for various newspapers, including my alma mater's campus publication, I have made quite a few game predictions in my short career. Some have come true. Some have not, despite what I might have thought would happen. As they say, *that's* why you play the game—to see how it turns out, no matter your pregame predictions. I plan to keep playing hard in mine down to the very last second.

But just like game predictions, the process of living requires that we look at the data, evaluate the odds, and then either defy them or be defeated by them. At the moment, I am still defying the odds. No matter what happens, I want you—along with the whole world—to know that I am not defeated.

I am writing this story to explore what it means for anyone, but especially someone of my age, to leave a legacy. To make an impact on the world. I'm telling my story because it's the only one I have to tell in the time that I have to tell it. I'm pretty surprised that anyone wants to hear it, but I choose to humbly accept my role in telling it the best I can . . . while I can.

Yes, my story is about life and death—that is, living life to the fullest, even while you're facing death—but you really can't miss the sports in between. I love athletics, perhaps to the point of mild obsession. Who am I kidding? The only "mild" thing in my life is salsa. Regardless, my love of sports is probably the main reason you and I are sitting here with these pages right now. Everyone has their favorite teams, along with their least favorite teams. Before I share my favorites, you might want to make a commitment now to not put down this book out of protest, especially if you're an Indiana University or Ohio State fan.

For a few hours, whatever your shade of red may be, why don't we call a truce. Deal?

I am a Boilermaker in every way. My dad is a Purdue alumnus, as am I—a story we will unpack in due time. I also cheer for the Indianapolis Colts, the Indiana Pacers, and the Chicago Cubs; so yeah, it's pretty obvious that in most every way imaginable, I was made to be the underdog. My teams have definitely had their moments of triumph, but for the most part, it's not historically uncommon for a large number of our regular season games to be opportunities for major upsets.

Again, this story of sports—this seemingly minor thing nudged between these weighty topics of life and death—should not be dismissed. Sports has proven to be the divinely inspired vehicle that has carried us to this conversation in the first place—and that part of this story began with my favorite underdog: Purdue.

My situation may seem *like a long shot*, but this story is not solely about me alone—not *by a long shot*. You're going to hear other perspectives in this story as well—after all, this is not just about me. You see, this whole unpredictable mess is really a crazy story about all of us.

And now you are becoming a part of this story, too.

The reality is that I might not be around to finish writing these pages or hold the published version of this book in my hands. Graciously, my friends and family have captured much of what I want to say and have committed to finish writing this story so that my words and the things I want the world to know about life, faith, suffering, and community can still be heard even after I'm gone.

I want to tell you stories—good and bad—that have led me to experience more purpose, encouragement, and love than anyone I've ever known in this world. And though I hope that our circumstances are different, my life is just like yours. It's okay to be upset by the difficult things you face; that is human. But there is something I have experienced that is higher than humanity. Better than life. Stronger than death.

It is the hope found in God's divinely written story—one that many of us have never really fully heard. The ending hasn't yet happened, and the middle can really hurt . . . trust me, I know. But if we will listen, there is so much hope right here in the middle of all this hurt—hope experienced and expressed when you lean in to real community and real grace, even when you find them lying in a hospital bed next to your friends and family, watching your favorite team pull off the upset of the decade against your least favorite team.

For me, the best part is that even if I lose, I still win. I will pass away someday, but my legacy—and yours—can continue forever because there is a greater, higher story being written . . . if you just know where to look for it.

Let's look for it together.

CHAPTER 2

Overwhelmed by Underdogs

(Tony & Kelly)

O ur oldest son, Tyler Trent, was born on September 7, 1998. He was our pride and joy, a unique child in every way. He was certainly not perfect—"exceptional" would be an accurate descriptor for our lanky, spunky, brilliant little boy—a boy who became an exceptional young man.

Calling him our "little boy" would no doubt make him blush, but this is at least some of the fun you get to have when you're a parent. It might embarrass him, but we couldn't be prouder of the young man you are meeting in these pages. The truth is, ten books would not be enough for you to fully know everything about him, but fully knowing Tyler is not his goal for this project; neither is it ours.

Knowing him fully, including every big and small challenge he has faced, fought, won, lost, and suffered through in his short life—this level of intimacy is reserved for only a select few in his family. His little brothers are in this club, as are his grandparents—and we are like the presidents of the club. Besides God himself, we saw it all, or at least as much as any other human not named Tyler Trent could witness.

Witnessing Tyler's life firsthand in all its glory—and all its gore—

has been one of the highest honors we will ever be given in this life. We got to walk through it all with him, sharing the highs and the lows. But at times, it has also been an almost unbearable weight, even though it has been our hearts' deepest desire to help carry it *with*—and sometimes *for*—our little boy. We never wanted him to feel alone, and we're confident that he never did.

As he continues to tell you his story, we have a few thoughts to add here and there—a different perspective on a journey that could not have been told fully through short interviews and features on ESPN or *Good Morning America*. There is so much more about our family's journey through the wins and losses that these incredibly kind and generous reports about our son could never capture or communicate. After all, most everyone else's vantage points of Tyler's story are views from a distance. Even if they are fairly good seats, they are still in the stands.

But we were joyfully, painfully close—and not just on the sidelines; we were *in* this game with Tyler. In the huddle with him. Blocking for him. Picking him up off the turf again and again as he took hit after brutal hit. To be quite honest, in some ways we feel just as beat up as he was; after all, we are his team.

So to be completely candid, it would be easier not to share our perspectives on this story. However, our dear Tyler was a writer at heart, dreaming of becoming a professional writer after college. During his final year of life, he developed a new goal: to write a book. So here we are in these pages, even though our parental hearts have been shattered into pieces over this story. But just as Tyler was never alone, neither have we been alone, even when we felt like it in emotional moments when illusions of isolation got the best of us.

Yet even then, the same faith and community that somehow sustained—and even strengthened Tyler as he simultaneously grew physically weaker—met us in our weakness as well. We have so many reasons to mourn, but we also have so much for which to be grateful. Grace wasn't just given to our son; it was given to us and continues to trickle down upon us as well.

And we're taking it the best we can.

Tyler's story is our story. You could no more separate the two than you could pull the sunshine out of the sun or a single shadow out of the darkness. Ironically, we've seen our fair share of both—a lot of sunshine and a lot of shadows on this journey with Tyler and our other two sons, Ethan and Blake.

So September 7, 1998, was the day our journey in this world began with our firstborn, but there was a lot that happened between that day and these more recent days, when "Tyler Trent" somehow inexplicably became a household name. For now, let's fast-forward to about twenty years and six weeks past his birth to one of the most satisfying moments of his young life. Honestly, it was also one of the most satisfying moments in our lives as well. It was also one of the moments God used to create this massive wave that has propelled this story to millions around the nation who have somehow joined hands across stadiums and social media platforms to proclaim themselves "Tyler Strong."

This moment was when Tyler accurately predicted the outcome of the 2018 Purdue game against Ohio State.

Tyler was the ultimate sports fanatic—a diligent studier and keeper of obscure dates and statistics. If it happened somewhere in sports history, Tyler probably knew about it and could quote it to you with an eerie level of accuracy.

You see, even before his diagnosis of bone cancer at the age of fifteen and his rise to notoriety, Tyler was no ordinary teenager. He was the kind of kid who absorbed and mastered most everything that came his way. A stellar student who read dozens of books each summer, he was also always the life of the party—a fun-loving friend known for his positive attitude and winning smile.

In fact, he was so positive and wore a smile so often that his childhood nickname eventually became "Smiley." He loved to smile that much. In many ways, as you will see, the brutal way cancer attempted to rob the smile from such a brilliant, beautiful boy is so much more evidence of the epic nature of his upset. As Tyler would agree, the best games are played between the strongest opponents. Tyler wasn't always strong, but he never completely lost the strength that mattered—because he found it *outside* himself.

Tyler was a whiz kid when it came to school, and this lasted all the way to college. As a freshman at Purdue, Tyler became a sports writer for the university newspaper, *The Exponent*. He was no stranger to the team, its players, or its coaches, having spent many afternoons working "on the beat," interviewing them after games and practices.

Completely bald from the chemo that was ravaging his body and propped up on crutches at the time, Tyler never acknowledged his cancer when he was doing his job—the job he was so gifted to do. The players and coaches never pointed it out, either; they were too busy answering his professional, probing questions concerning their latest change in system, play calling, or personnel. Sure, they would ask him how he was doing, but always off the record, as friends.

But by this particular game day during his sophomore year, Tyler was no longer covering the team as he did when he first moved into his dorm at Tarkington Hall on Purdue's West Lafayette campus. He simply didn't have the strength to do so.

But he did have something else to offer: a bold prediction.

This was nothing new for our son—he always pushed the limits. The now-famous ESPN video of Tyler's interview with Tom Rinaldi, a correspondent for ESPN and ABC, shows him writhing in pain, yet boldly predicting that his beloved Boilermakers would pull off the upset against a vastly superior Ohio State Buckeyes football team. Millions of people watched this story around the world—and the *TylerStrong* movement that had already spread across Indiana went nationwide for reasons beyond what most people know or would expect. After all, there are so many people out there who suffer from cancer, including innocent children.

Why this young man, who happened to be our son? Why this moment?

A simple scroll through the comments left on any of the many videos posted about Tyler at least begins to reveal the answers to these questions. Kids and parents of terminally ill children have posted videos and pictures of their own "Tylers," thanking him for his courage to speak up, to keep going, and to defy the odds with his courageous boldness. We feel for these other families—we know what they are going through.

But quite frankly, Tyler's prediction of a Purdue victory over the Buckeyes was about as farfetched as his own meager odds against osteosarcoma. Again, Tyler loved to research and acknowledge the statistics, then defy them . . . in style.

We knew what the world didn't: that Tyler had predicted the upset long before that ESPN piece took his story viral. He let his unorthodox sentiments be heard months earlier on one of the many sports podcasts on which he was often featured. And make no mistake, he was always being interviewed primarily because of his in-depth knowledge of his team, their opposition, and the ensuing minutiae of their offensive and defensive matchups. His cancer was always a follow-up question.

Because he was an expert, few were shocked when he predicted that his Boilermakers squad would finish the season with at least an even record of six wins and six losses, qualifying for their first bowl game in years. But his opinion became somewhat scandalous when he also said that, along the way, Purdue would also pull off the upset over Ohio State.

"Excuse me?" was the response that came from the interviewer.

That was when Tyler knew he had really put himself out there publicly. But like so many things in his life, he decided to stick to his guns, no matter what the odds. After all, odds—and upsetting them—were kind of his thing.

When the anticipated day arrived for the game in Indiana, ESPN's *College GameDay* was being shot on a set across the country in Pullman, Washington, where the twenty-fifth ranked Washington State Cougars were slated to face the visiting twelfth-ranked Oregon Ducks. Amid the many predictions from the ESPN personalities about the multiple games being played that day, the frantic cheering of the fans behind them, and the hilarious homemade signs that serve as a trademark for the famous show, there was a pause in the programing to air Tyler's story to the nation.

Tom Rinaldi and an ESPN production crew had already spent a lot of time with us that week. They had also interviewed Purdue players, coaches, and other friends and family members, splicing together a powerful video scrapbook of Tyler's incredible life story and struggle. We were so proud, but even we could feel that something else—something much more significant—was happening in these moments.

In that video, Tyler's garbled words were fairly difficult to understand, but his audacious prediction was clearly articulated: "Purdue will beat Ohio State." In that moment, as one great underdog picked another great underdog to win, the nation became overwhelmed by the story of a boy—well, a young man—whom we had been admiring for two decades. His great boldness, demonstrated in both his love for sports and his love for what matters most in life, was now on full display.

At that time, what everyone—including those of us in his family—did not know was that some of Tyler's extremely belabored speech was due to the fact that he was suffering from life-threatening complications caused by an excessive number of surgeries, paralysis, and treatment. The full picture of his medical journey was not always pretty. Tyler began experiencing seizures during his sophomore year that paralyzed the left side of his body, along with everything below his waist.

At that particular point, his kidneys also began to shut down due to all the chemotherapy his body had absorbed, so his doctors had surgically installed nephrostomy tubes to improve his kidney functions. This entailed making two incisions into his lower back and pushing tubes down into his kidneys so they could drain. What none of us knew as ESPN interviewed us that week was that there was a problem with the tubes. They were causing his kidneys to back up and were putting his life in grave danger. The night after Tyler shot his famous interview, we were in the hospital with him as he underwent an emergency surgery to repair his nephrostomy tubes in an attempt to get his kidneys functioning again.

What happened next still breaks our hearts to this day. They gave Tyler anesthesia for the surgery, but as can happen in rare cases, it only rendered him unable to communicate, but he could still feel pain! He lay there during the surgery trying to communicate—to scream out in agony because he could feel everything that was happening to him—but was unable to do so. Afterward, he told us that it was the most pain he had ever experienced in his life. It wrecked us!

Tyler spent the week recovering the best he could, but he was still facing a litany of complications—almost as if each treatment was somehow tipping some invisible scale disproportionately in the wrong direction. It felt like every time a problem was addressed, a new one emerged from the process . . . endless problems somehow being caused by solutions. This is a frustrating feature of fighting cancer that we know many patients and their families face every day.

Needless to say, those few days were nothing short of physically and emotionally exhausting for Tyler—and for us. So by the time the Friday before the OSU game rolled around, we thought we might be done—meaning, we thought Tyler might be at the end. He was now suffering from debilitating migraine headaches, along with constant bouts of nausea and vomiting. At that point, we were just hoping he would survive the weekend because we knew how much watching the Purdue game would mean to him.

Trying to sleep when your child is clinging to life is an impossibility. It is torture—like a nocturnal purgatory that seemingly never ends. You just want your boy to make it. To stop hurting. To get better. So our focus was on his sleep, not ours. We spent the night near our boy, nodding off occasionally from the sheer exhaustion we were feeling, but mostly just keeping vigil, as we had done multiple times before.

But as the night passed, something truly miraculous happened.

The next morning, Tyler woke up feeling significantly better. It was a night and day difference. We had the distinct feeling that morning that this wasn't just a happenstance upturn. Rather, it felt as if God had mercifully breathed a little bit of life into our boy. He was himself—still a very sick young man, but not falling over the edge as he had been the whole week before. He was talking about football. He was talking about writing a book. He was dreaming again.

We were all shocked, but we were even more grateful. Any extra moments with our son felt like extra presents under the Christmas tree. But just feeling better wasn't enough—Tyler made it clear to all of us that he felt good enough to go to the game.

Of course he did.

From a parental standpoint, our first inclination was to leave well enough alone—to keep him in bed and make him rest. But we had learned that Tyler had no interest in merely surviving; he was going to live every moment he was alive. And he was going to do so with or without our permission. Somewhere along the line, we made the conscious decision not to do anything that would ever make him feel we were trying to slow down his drive to live life to the fullest, even as he was dying.

Sure, this made for an extremely complicated existence because navigating a terminally ill, almost completely disabled person with all his medicine, equipment, and supplies through airports, rush-hour traffic, and the like—with two other teenage boys in tow, mind you—was not exactly the most efficient, convenient, or easiest way to travel.

But this was *our life*—helping Tyler live *his life*.

As we faced an unexpected journey together that foggy Saturday morning, even Tyler—with all his wild predictions—couldn't have possibly forecast what other miracles awaited us, both on and off the field.

As the sun illuminated the Indiana sky on the afternoon of October 20, our own underdog yet again overwhelmed the odds as we all headed out to the big game—a game where Tyler's name would be affectionately chanted by tens of thousands of people, where other underdogs in similar situations would find their own stronger voices through his weakened voice, and where his friends who had suited up in black and gold to face the second-ranked, undefeated football team in the nation were facing their own uphill climb toward an upset.

CHAPTER 3

A Stadium-Sized Experience

(Tyler)

The fact that I could attend the Purdue game against Ohio State was nothing less than a dream come true, especially because I had almost died a few days before. I know that attending a football game may seem pretty insignificant when you're facing death, but for me, it was about so much more than mere fandom or another sports experience; it was about being present with the players, coaches, university classmates, and community who had joined my biological loved ones in becoming family to me.

I also wanted to follow through on my commitment as an honorary co-captain of the Purdue Boilermakers. Was this the ideal time to go to an athletic event? Obviously not. But it's always an ideal time to follow through on your commitments. My dad has always used an expression that sticks with me to this day and factors heavily into much of my story. It is short and simple, but profound for understanding priorities.

If you don't have time, make time.

I knew I probably did not have much time left here on this earth, so I wasn't going to miss this opportunity to make time for those who mattered so much to me. Alongside them, I wanted to experience everything this day would bring. Plus, I knew we would win, so who would want to miss the biggest upset of the season?

Here's the thing about being terminal: a strange freedom accompanies your life when you're living at full throttle while you can, even though you know it is temporary. I have been blessed with parents and a family who have accepted this reality, as painful as it has been for them to accept. We have chosen to do everything we can, even though our "entourage" is like some weird traveling medical circus, minus the trapezes and the elephants . . . except that one big elephant somehow finds a way to always stay in the room: the fact that I have a terminal illness.

My family does all this for me anyway because they don't just love me to death; they also love me to life. I'm eternally thankful for their willingness to do so—I know it is far from easy.

Riding in Secret Style

Because this particular Saturday was the biggest game of the year, as well as the moment when my crazy prediction would either make me look like a sports genius or—more likely—like some wacko cancer patient out of his mind on pain medications, there was no way we were staying home and watching the game on ESPN. We were going to this game—and it would prove to be one of the most incredible experiences of our lives.

Perhaps the best place to begin is with the way it all felt. No doubt, my most memorable impression was the unbelievable level of care and attention shown to me and my family. And it began with a Secret Service escort.

I kid you not.

A Secret Service agent attended our church, and one of our youth leaders contacted him about my situation. I don't know the exact conversation they had, but it must have been significant.

The Secret Service was conducting extensive pre-event preparations for the game. Because it was such a huge, sold-out event, it was also a possible target for terrorists, as any large public gathering might be these days. Agents had spent the week training the West Lafayette Police Department, helping them sweep the stadium area for bombs and other dangers. The agent from our church had been in constant communication with his superiors and counterparts that week.

At first, the agent felt it would be helpful—and also fun—to escort us in a Secret Service vehicle to the game, with full lights, sirens, and the whole shebang. Graciously considering my medical condition, from a practical standpoint, an escort would help us make it through all the game-day traffic much quicker and easier. But unfortunately, the agency would not approve use of the government vehicle for such a purpose.

As it turns out, I'm not the president.

But they were able to do the next best thing: one agent rode along with us in our car to ensure that everything went smoothly for us on the drive in, while another awaited our arrival at the stadium. Police checkpoints had been set up all around the area, complete with search dogs and detection equipment to sweep vehicles for weapons or bombs. Everyone was required to stop and wait to be searched—everyone, that is, except us. After all, we had our very own Secret Service agent already securing our vehicle, radioing ahead to tell "the powers that be" to let us through. What could have taken at least an hour instead took only a few minutes. We were able to just drive up to the stadium entrance to be dropped off.

That day, two Secret Service agents stayed with me everywhere I went. They stood silently nearby with their hands clasped in front of them, as if they were guarding a visiting dignitary or a prime minister. This was not just some publicity stunt; in fact, if they ever read this, I imagine they will be displeased with the press. Regardless, these heroes who are highly trained to step in front of a speeding bullet to save someone else obviously took the act of "guarding" my family and me very seriously, although obviously no one would want to hurt us. It was one of the most special and surreal experiences of my life, an experience that few people will ever have. These heroes were simply standing in line with the other million unexpected blessings God has used to comfort me along this very painful path, reminding me that I'm not alone—and more importantly, that I'm loved.

The Other Side of the Camera

A camera crew from ESPN followed us all the way from our house to the stadium. Of course, Tom Rinaldi's piece on my story had aired that morning—and apparently, *everyone* in the whole world had already seen it not just once, but twice—at least that's how it felt because Twitter was blowing up before my very eyes.

Furthermore, it had been publicized on our local media that I was definitely going to the game. So when the agents opened the car door to drop us off, we were met with a flurry of cameras, flashing lights, reporters—and crowds of cheering people who were acting like fans.

At that point, because many local and regional news outlets had interviewed me about my story, I was not a stranger to the media. Also, as a sports reporter, I had spent quite a bit of time on the other side of the cameras. But this was different—and by different, I mean insane. I remember thinking, *Well, I guess this is how famous people feel.* I was rolled through the stadium concourse in a wheelchair while people all around me screamed my name and asked for my autograph. Many of them were holding "TylerStrong" signs. I would soon discover that countless other people throughout the student section and other parts of the stadium were holding their own signs as well. It was unbelievable to me that someone would take the time to make a sign for me.

Once inside the stadium, we made our way up the elevators to a special suite near the press area, near the top floor. It was a cold evening—way too cold for me to sit outside, so I was graciously invited to watch the game in the Purdue Center For Cancer Research suite. I was the first student ever given the incredible honor of being invited to serve on the board for the Purdue Center For Cancer Research. It has been an unbelievable privilege that has afforded me more opportunities to speak up and speak out on the issue of cancer, advocating for other victims and their families in the struggle to find a cure for this horrible disease. After we had finally made it through the loving barrage of media and fans to the room, it was finally time for the big game—the moment I had been waiting for the most.

When I saw my Boilermakers run out onto the field, I broke down crying. I didn't think I was even going to be alive the night before, yet there I was, sitting with my family in this incredible room, feeling deeply loved by Boiler Nation. You may have seen me cry in the first big ESPN video that broke my story, but I'm not someone who becomes emotional very easily. When that video was shot, I was heavily medicated, which sometimes makes it difficult for me to control my emotions. On most normal days, it has always been a pretty big deal for me to cry.

This was no normal day, though.

The kickoff ensued, and the game finally began. I was in Boilermaker heaven. But all evening long, loving interruptions came and went from our suite. Reporters. University staff and personnel. Local government officials. The university president. ESPN personalities and crew. Purdue fans. And yes, even Ohio State fans. Tom Rinaldi and his camera crew also joined me on and off throughout the game. He is a uniquely kind and gracious man, and I thoroughly enjoyed the time we spent speaking with each other between visits from other people.

So even with all the hoopla leading up to that moment, I didn't get to focus much on watching the game from start to finish. Normally, this would really bother me—after all, very few things come between me and my Purdue football and live to tell about it. But on this night, I didn't mind so much.

Kirk Herbstreit, an analyst for ESPN's *College GameDay*, was doing the color commentary for the game on ESPN. At one point, I sent a note to him. We had never officially met, so I asked him if he would mind stepping over during halftime from the media booth to say hello. He had already shown such kindness to me in various correspondences, and I wanted to thank him in person.

He sent an extremely kind note back to me, saying he had already been so moved by my story that he worried if he met me in person right then, he might not be able to compose himself enough to get through the second half of the broadcast. He promised a future meeting soon, but his personal concern and emotion for me touched my heart so very deeply in that moment. He kept his promise, calling me on the phone and later even awarding me the "Herbie," his own personal award given to the most inspirational person in college football. This is the same level of heartfelt compassion I have felt from so many of the ESPN personalities and staff.

It seems strange to me that I have said so much about the experience without mentioning what seemingly should be the most incredible part of the whole story—the score of the game. I guess that's what happens when you experience monumental moments of grace with people—love eclipses everything else. Even so, when Tom Rinaldi and I chatted off-camera, the main topic we discussed was the seemingly impossible fact that Purdue was not only *beating* Ohio State, but *pounding* them. It wasn't even close. By midway through the third quarter, the Boilermakers were leading 21 to 6.

Yes, a team barely above .500 was soundly trouncing the mighty undefeated, top-ten Buckeyes. The Boilermakers would go on to score 28 more points in the fourth quarter alone, eventually winning the game 49 to 20.

It wasn't just an upset; it was a "Hammer Down."

As the end of the fourth quarter came into sight, we made our way down to the field. As I was rolled out onto the sidelines, I experienced something I will never forget: everyone in the entire stadium stood up and began cheering for me.

Let that sink in. These faithful Boilermakers fans were witnessing the greatest upset they had experienced in years—the resurgence of a struggling football program—but it felt like the most important thing to them wasn't football; it was being present and supportive in my suffering.

In that moment, instead of feeling surrounded by all the anxiety that cancer can bring, I felt surrounded by something else—love.

CHAPTER 4

Surrounded

(Tony & Kelly)

The personal connection to all things Purdue began when Tony was a little kid. He grew up about thirty-five miles from West Lafayette in a very rural area—and he always dreamed of going to Purdue. He knew stories of the glory days of Bob Griese quarterbacking the mighty Boilermakers and Gene Keady coaching the basketball team to greatness, so a deep fondness for Purdue University just seemed to be in his blood.

Tyler must have inherited this love of sports. Ever since he was knee-high to a grasshopper, he immersed himself in all things athletics. We still have a huge container of football and baseball cards in our attic from the days when he would spend hours collecting and meticulously organizing them—with Tyler, the details really mattered.

He always loved watching games of any kind. Before he became sick, watching a football game was quite the affair. He would yell at the TV—and at coaches and referees through the TV—as if they could hear him. But his wasn't just rabid fandom; he would meticulously come up with his own game plan, including what plays should be called. If only the many coaches he yelled at could have heard him—they probably would have won more games.

Talk about being "upset"—this kid would lose his mind over the outcome of a game or series. He was always a loyal fan—well, really a loyal person. Once he bought into something, he was all in.

So the day of the Ohio State upset was extra special for all of us because we knew that it meant so much to him.

It almost seemed like a providential moment for Tyler to get to say one last good-bye to Purdue and for Purdue to say one last good-bye to him. We will never forget the moment that the longstanding—perhaps not so classy, but still hilarious—Purdue tradition of yelling "IU Sucks" at every kickoff (regardless of the opponent) was changed for that one game. For Tyler, the whole stadium instead chanted, "Cancer sucks!" I (Tony) reached down and touched Tyler on the shoulder. I said, "Tyler, that's for you."

The chant was obviously for Tyler, but it was also for us. People have no idea how a kind gesture or an encouraging word can make all the difference between feeling like you can't make it another day and surviving to see tomorrow. This is the incredible power that a loving community can have on a suffering family. Sure, people's kind words can't change our situation—cancer has been our reality. But people's kindness *can* change the way we are dealing with our situation for at least one moment.

We know it might seem farfetched for some, but to us, this experience had to be at least a small taste of the exhilarating feeling we will have in heaven. We have never felt anything like it in our lives. For a moment, everything seemed perfect. All the people were in unison. The best way to explain it is that it was magical.

One OSU fan standing by their section walked down to where we were and asked me (Tony) if we had any more of the yellow wristbands like the one I was wearing. It was a "Tyler Strong" wristband, the one that many members of the team, including quarterback David Blough, wore during every game. I graciously told the man that I had only my own and that I never take it off. Just then, one of my old friends who was with me, Mark Walpole, took off his own wristband and gave it to the man, who smiled as if he had received the best Christmas gift ever given.

This was the aura that surrounded the whole game—incredible

moments of peace and generosity in Tyler's life, and in ours as well. From the locker-room speech to the thousands of well-wishers, our family experienced something truly miraculous and undeserved. For just a moment, we were able to breathe—to take it all in and not think about the way everything would someday end. For a moment, we joined in with a community of people cheering not just for football, but for something much more personal—for our son.

This is probably the reason why we had so much trouble going to sleep that night. We didn't want the experience to end, just as we never wanted our time with Tyler to end, either. It was during this time that a connection seemed to form somewhere in our minds between the Purdue football season and Tyler's journey. We thought the journey was about to be over—as did Tyler's doctors—but God had some unfinished business ahead for our super-fan son.

We have often said that the moment Tyler was diagnosed with cancer, we all got cancer. This is because everything he went through, we went through with him, just in different ways. Throughout the entire journey—which we are still processing and healing from—cancer tried to destroy us as much as it tried to destroy Tyler.

We say this not to gain sympathy, but simply to let the world know that families dealing with cancer are facing an uphill battle that goes far beyond just the physical suffering. It can feel isolating, even when you're surrounded by people. So while people's kind words can't "snap you out" of the darkness and make everything okay, they can remind you—in a moment when you feel isolated or forgotten—that you are still remembered.

We needed to be reminded—and we still do.

Every human being needs to feel loved and validated. For a family, cancer is an extremely lonely journey. People often don't know how to respond to what you're facing because they take a level of psychological ownership over your situation. In other words, they take what's happening to your child and hypothetically put it on their child—imagining themselves in your shoes—and this level of empathy freaks them out so badly that it becomes easier for them to keep their distance, or at least maintain silence, than to offer words of comfort.

Take it from people who have been there: you don't have to know what to say—just be present and say *something*. Avoid trying to rationalize or even spiritualize the situation, and avoid making grand, sweeping statements that try to explain what's happening. If you do choose to share a scripture, which can be helpful, do so with a tone of shared brokenness and humility, not piety or spiritual superiority. The right verse shared in the right moment can be very helpful, but religious dismissiveness can inflict pain.

People in crisis don't need any Mr. or Mrs. Fix-Its, who can do more harm than good. Just try to be present and be prayerful. These gestures are so simple yet so important because one person's intentional presence with no intention of "fixing" or making darkness into sunshine can help validate deep feelings of loneliness, even if those feelings are difficult to verbalize.

Our journey has felt like we've been running a hundred marathons. If you've ever participated in a marathon, then perhaps you know the power of people standing by the road and cheering you on as you pass by. Their presence can truly encourage you to make it another mile.

The writer of Hebrews knew this to be true as well, which is why he used this exact illustration in encouraging us to finish the race before us. He referred to the fact that we are "surrounded by a great cloud of witnesses"—these are people, past and present, who are standing on the road cheering us on toward the finish line. Their encouragement is our necessity in running "with endurance the race that is set before us" (Hebrews 12:1, ESV).

Jesus also faced a difficult race during his time on Earth, though he was certainly capable of doing anything he wanted at any time he wanted. Yet even he chose to not run the race alone. He avoided isolation and lived honestly and openly in community with twelve other guys, leaning on them for encouragement and asking them repeatedly to be present with him and to pray with him.

In good moments and in bad, we have come to believe that no one can survive alone. Some people treat this truth as if it is optional, but take it from a family with cancer—it is not. Again, even Jesus didn't want to go it alone.

God made us not just for friendship, but for deep, honest, authentic—even seemingly intrusive—community with people we can truly trust . . . people who will both stand on the sidelines and cheer us forward and step in to pick us up off the pavement when we trip, stumble, and face-plant. Maybe that's why the stadium felt a little like heaven. Heaven will also feature a "great cloud of witnesses" to this race of life—those whose lives and prayers helped cheer us on when we felt like we couldn't move another inch.

Just as we felt a tiny bit of heaven when we were surrounded by the encouragement of community, our bet is that you know someone who could use a little glimpse of heaven, too. You can help reveal it by just being present and prayerful in their situation. When you are sitting in what feels like hell, momentary glimpses of heaven make all the difference.

They can bring moments of life to moments when all you can see is death.

CHAPTER 5

Love and Locker Rooms

(Tyler)

As I looked around, I noticed that a large number of Ohio State faithful were standing and directing their cheers toward the sidelines—toward me. Not to go all sports geek on you, but bear with me—we spoiled Ohio State's season that night. When it all shook out, our win was their lone loss of the season—the lone loss that kept the college football brass from letting OSU into the four-team college playoff at the end of the season.

The Buckeyes were left on the outside looking in, and this would also prove to be the last season their legendary coach, Urban Meyer, would call football plays professionally. He announced his retirement after the season. Without this loss, the Buckeyes would have remained undefeated, made the playoffs, and possibly been on their way to another national championship.

Even so, many of the Ohio State fans sitting in the section near where we were standing said things to us like, "If there was one game we had to lose, we're glad it was this one. We love you, Tyler!"

The whole experience was just more evidence of the greater upset that God was divinely brewing through my unlikely story—a story I've been permitted to live, and yes, to suffer through. It was nothing less than pure beauty in the middle of ashes. It was light in the middle of shadows. The loud support of this stadium crammed full of strangers-made-friends reminded me that I wasn't alone.

It also reminded me that countless other loved ones and children out there facing their own matchups with cancer might just experience more love and support as a result of people's hearts being moved to action in these moments of unity. Because awareness is so critical to those who are facing this disease, it has long been my hope that moments like these in my story will let others' stories be heard more clearly and celebrated.

The love in the stadium that night reflected that which truly shines brighter than athletics. Stronger than regional or university rivalries. Longer than records or championships. Higher than fame, fortune, or accolades.

As the game came down to the last two minutes, "my" Secret Service detail (as I now refer to them) began to become more than a little concerned about my safety because the field was about to be flooded with media, fans, and players from the sidelines. So they ushered me off the field and into the locker room, where the Purdue team and coaches would soon join me after their on-field celebrations and interviews.

Little did I know what would happen next.

A Different Kind of Locker-Room Talk

After their on-field celebration began to subside, the Purdue team, coaches, and staff began pouring into the locker room. When they saw me, they began giving me high fives, cheering, and celebrating *their* huge upset with me as if it was *our* win.

To them, it truly was *our* win.

They treated me as if I had been out on the field with them all night. Again, I had been named one of the honorary captains for that game, but the enthusiastic reception they gave me in the locker room was far from just honorary in the technical or ceremonial sense. It was authentic. With tears in their eyes, numerous players and coaches—including my dear friend, senior quarterback David Blough—continuously patted me on the shoulder. In a chaotic chorus, many leaned in one by one to speak or whisper in my ear.

"You inspired us to do this!"

"We couldn't have done it without you!"

"This is truly your win, not just ours!"

It would have been easy to dismiss their words as merely kind sentiments, but I could tell that they really meant it, so I really accepted their loving statements. Coach Brohm finally made his way into the middle of the room and attempted to temporarily tame the room. He opened his "locker speech" as follows: "I know you guys know who our new team captain is. Tyler Trent, right here."

The room again erupted with thunderous cheering, none of which I felt I deserved. Coach Brohm continued, "As you guys know, 'Tyler Strong' means something. This young man has been strong. His family has been strong. We're happy as heck to support him and have him as our team captain. For him to even be here is remarkable. The guy never makes excuses. He never complains. He has a huge smile on his face every day. He has a great attitude. He's about giving back to other people—and that's really what being a Boilermaker is all about."

To say I was moved by Coach Brohm's words would be the understatement of the century, but I didn't have much time to think about it before the next unexpected experience came my way. Coach quieted them again, and then he asked me to address the locker room. That's something that in a million years, I never thought I would ever be doing following the largest upset in modern school history.

What does one say in such a moment? I tried to keep it short and sweet: "Thanks for leaving your heart out on the field and showing the nation what being a Boilermaker is really all about." They again erupted into cheers. After the noise died back down, I continued with one last hopeful—but highly practical—sentiment.

"And hopefully, ESPN does us right and puts us at number twenty-five."

For the record, despite my rousing locker-room speech and my highly publicized call for a higher ranking for Purdue, ESPN did not heed my completely unbiased counsel.

I wish I could have stayed in that moment forever. With my family. With my Boilermaker brothers. With the big win behind me and nothing but hope ahead—or at least that's how it felt for a brief moment. I was living in the very definition of an upset, but unfortunately, no single moment in this life is permanent. Still, I lingered there as long as I could until it was finally time to go home. Back to my hospice bed. Back to my prognosis. Back to a bleak outlook, from a physical standpoint.

The Power of Sports

In case you're wondering, I have been asked a lot of hard questions about how people facing my kind of situation can possibly find such huge value in something as seemingly insignificant as sports. At the end of the day, the technical value of a game is truly nothing, yet it can produce something worth so much more. It's easy to see why, for many athletes and fans, sports are a reflection of life.

But where does the value of sports really come from? From the people—people like one of my former high school teachers, Maggie Smith, who of her own accord organized a grassroots GoFundMe campaign to send me and my friend, Jake Heinzman, to Santa Clara, California, in December 2017 to watch Purdue beat Arizona in the Foster Farms Bowl. I mean, who does that? People do . . . and when these kinds of people engage in sports, the sports community has and will continue to do so much good in this world.

This level of generosity affects me so deeply. I was blessed to grow up in an environment where if you wanted something, you were encouraged to work for it. My brothers and I learned the value of hard work. I have held a job since I was fourteen years old. After all, there were things I wanted—like a car and a college experience. If I wanted it, then I needed to work for it. Work ethic was one of the most valuable gifts my parents ever gave me.

So for me, the fact that people donate their hard-earned money—money they have spent long days and long nights working for—just wrecks me. It's not their money they're giving, but rather themselves. They give freely to me—and to others like me who suffer from cancer—just so that we might be able to attend a silly game, which, at the end of the day, doesn't amount to anything but a win or a loss.

But for people like me, it becomes more than just a win or a loss. It's about being unified with others and experiencing the highs and lows together for four quarters. For me, it also helps to take my mind off the daily pain.

I use sports as an illustration because it has played such a huge role in my story. Through sports, I have been supported and encouraged more times than I can count when I've been down. I think sports—and athletics in general—has a really cool ability to do this for people, especially when someone is facing a crisis similar to mine.

Sports are a mirror of the people who play them, organize them, report about them, coach them, and ultimately watch them. A sport can be just a hobby, but it can also be a community. After all, if no one participates in a sport in any of the ways I have described, it won't be a sport for long.

In other words, sports not only reflect people . . . they *are* people.

It's not the throwing of a ball or the act of jumping, running, or sprinting that gives sports the life they seem to possess outside of just rules or outcomes. A sport *without* people would be nothing more than an inanimate collection of rules and equipment; but a sport *with* people creates events where life happens. This life can be negative, as evidenced by individual or even citywide social media vitriol, or even violence, which sometimes breaks out when a certain team wins over another. Yes, it can also be the wrong kind of distraction—one that keeps parents from spending time with their children or renders them inattentive and unproductive at work, especially during midweek golf tournaments or the NCAA tournament.

Again, a sport without people would be inanimate—and like anything that is inanimate, what you do with it determines its positive or negative value. A cake isn't inherently good or bad; it's how much of it you choose to eat in one sitting that determines whether you will be blissfully full or sick to your stomach. The way we use athletics determines the way it either improves or detracts from our lives.

To this end, I have discovered some incredibly gracious people out there in the sports world, from professionals to players to fans, who are using sports for incredibly good purposes. They have enriched the remaining time I have on this earth, however long it lasts. They have offered one-of-a-kind experiences that can at least distract a person from other one-of-a-kind experiences he wishes weren't happening to him. Cancer. Loss. Pain.

Athletics has played a huge role in my story. It is one of the bridges across which an immeasurable amount of love has come into my life. Take Purdue, for instance. The university, athletic department, coaches, players, staff, students, and fans have stood by me in ways I could never imagine someone doing in a million years—and in ways that I will still be remembering a million years from now. Their outpouring of love and support is something I would have never expected.

Honestly, I can barely write about it without becoming very emotional . . . and this is not just the medication talking.

There's really no way to quantify how much it affected me when Dabo Swinney paused his insane schedule to send me a signed football and then called me on the phone. Or Adam Vinatieri stopping by my house just to talk to me and spend time with me. Or the seniors from the Purdue football team coming to my house to present me with the game ball from the 2018 Nebraska game and then asking if they could pray for me. All of this is nothing less than the grace of God demonstrated in the lives of normal people. I sit here in this moment right now, legitimately astounded by it.

When cancer gets old, love never does.

It is my hope that this book will challenge more people to be the "life" in sports or in any other bridge that spans the distance between people's circumstances and the hope they so desperately need to experience. I hope you will pay forward to others the encouragement I have received, especially to those facing life-threatening conditions or diseases.

Hope Inextinguishable

When you are in hospice care and unsure how many days you have left, these gestures of kindness truly breathe extra life into your emotional lungs. I had a friend with cancer who wanted to be the general manager for a certain professional basketball team, so the organizational leaders went out of their way to make him GM for a day. It was impactful and fun—and its impact lasted much, much longer than a day. It was a moment he constantly revisited in his mind whenever he needed a boost of joy in the middle of his despair.

I went home after Purdue's upset to face what was next, but I did not go home alone, and certainly I did not go home without hope.

My hope was rekindled that day. A kind of hope that holds strong, both when we win and when we lose. A hope that can't be extinguished by cancer, chemo, or college football rankings.

Hopelessness can feel so real, but it is a mirage. Sure, my cancer is real. My terminal diagnosis is real. My hope is not a denial of these realities; rather, my hope is based on something more real than these realities. I am facing death, and it is absolutely a formidable opponent, but I know that my death will not be a reflection of death's final ranking—that is, death itself has already been beaten. Death cannot wrestle *true* life away from the one who trusts—even in weakness—in Jesus, the only one who took death to overtime and beyond, emerging from the grave a winner.

Please do not mistake my use of sports metaphors as if I am dismissing the suffering we all face, or as if I am all too neatly summing up the human condition. On the contrary, I am suffering immensely right now *from* the human condition, and the physical component experiencing this condition—my physical body—will probably not survive.

But I am not only physical. I have been adopted into a higher family, and by the rules of that holy household, my eventual death *here* only means my eternal life *there*.

I realize that you may or may not share the same "faith" background as I do—and that's okay. I also realize that I'm just a twenty-year-old, and you very well may be much older, much more educated, or have more life experiences. I also acknowledge that you may have negative feelings toward religious or faith-based things, questions about theology or suffering in this world, or legitimate doubts about faith that my little story could never completely eradicate in a few pages.

I get it. If you're like me, you have valid reasons why you think the way you do. But let me make you a promise: I will not try to answer all the unanswerable questions with easy, quotable "gotcha" statements that dismiss doubts or sum up suffering with tidy bows. I'm not here to answer every religious question about suffering. All I can do is write about the hope I have in Christ —a hope that has carried me through my darkest moments. So if you struggle with faith, please don't throw away my story just because I'm a broken man who also believes and has hope.

I'm still so very broken.

I'm not *that* guy—the one who has it all figured out. Who never doubts. Who always prays. Who never loses heart. The truth is, I have paralyzing doubts, and I don't always feel like praying. No, a lot of what I'm about to tell you will be difficult to communicate. I have fallen hard. I have lost the faith. I have blown it, but hope has always sought me out again. It's always been there beneath the surface of my circumstance.

I have also been picked up. Forgiven when I have failed. Restored. I have been healed, even as cancer still seeks to kill me.

But cancer can only take my physical life—I have been given the gift of another kind of life. I didn't earn it. I'm not "good enough" to merit it. I don't keep it by never failing, but neither do I lose it by failing hard. It is very secure, more secure than my successes or my failures. It is stronger than me, and it hasn't budged, even when my diagnosis and my courage have both fluctuated wildly. It is the only kind of life that can give me a sense of hope in the face of death.

Speaking of death, I know it's kind of the elephant in the room— the fact that I may very well die before you can finish reading these words. Let me take you down the longer road of my story and show you the ways cancer has affected my family and me. Let me show you how my strength has been tested and found to be insufficient so many times, yet how I am still, somehow, standing today in the strength of another: our loving God.

CHAPTER 6

From Big Dreams to Bad Nightmares

(Tyler)

I still remember what it was like to be a kid.

I know that may sound strange to some people since I'm only a few years into my adulthood. But from a certain point forward, I don't think I was ever just "a kid." My childhood drastically changed while it was still happening.

There was a moment when this change occurred. An exact time. Odds are, if you can pinpoint a moment when you crossed over from adolescence into adulthood, that moment is probably not a good one.

Dreams

Most people have thousands of dreams spanning the course of thousands of nights of sleep, but they do not remember the majority of them. Most of our dreams are nothing but images passing through our brains containing snippets of our days, our values, our pursuits, and our worries, all crammed into what seems like random visual sequences. Most people have trouble remembering their dreams.

But most people have trouble forgetting their nightmares.

I was living the good life of a teenager, beginning to come into my own. I was on my way to a driver's license and the freedom of owning a car. High school can feel like an endless eternity while you're in it, but I was beginning to envision the end of it just ahead of me. Graduation. Girlfriends. College. Career. It was all beginning to materialize on the no-longer-so-distant horizon.

These were my teenage dreams. But before I could reach those dreams, I crashed headlong into a nightmare. It began sometime in May 2014, when I was still just a sophomore in high school. I was homeschooled from kindergarten all the way through to graduation. People make fun of me for being a homeschooler sometimes, but I don't really care—it was a great experience, and I had the most incredible teacher. (Shout-out to Mom.)

I loved the game of basketball, and I played in a homeschool league made up of various teams from other homeschool cooperatives, or co-ops, as they are often called. We were gearing up for basketball season that fall, but when I went out into the driveway to practice, I wasn't able to shoot the ball because my right arm was hurting so badly. The pain was severe, and it persisted for several weeks with little to no relief.

We just figured it was something muscular. I had obviously pulled some muscle in my arm from overuse or from lifting too much weight. With growing pains and just the random discomfort that comes with training—and with being a teenage guy during a growth spurt—this was the explanation that made the most sense at the time.

But the pain just wouldn't stop.

We mentioned my issue to our neighbor, who was a doctor. He graciously agreed to give me a very quick, very informal once-over. He said that without any medical imaging equipment, and from what he could tell by just feeling around on my arm, the most likely culprit was indeed probably something muscular. But as any good doctor would do, he told us that we should go see our family physician about it as soon as possible.

I was in no hurry to pause my busy life and head off to the doctor for something so minor. In the meantime, our neighbor gave me some exercises that we all hoped would loosen me up and get me through whatever this nagging injury was. They didn't seem to help, but I kept doing them anyway.

The summer kept unfolding, but the pain still wasn't going way. I tried to stay active doing the things I loved, which included playing Ultimate Frisbee.

My best friend since childhood is a knucklehead named Josh Seals—my more-than-willing partner in crime—that is, innocent adolescent hijinks and fun. It was his sixteenth birthday party in June, so I was at his house to celebrate with all our friends.

During his party, we went outside to play a game of Ultimate Frisbee. On the throw-off, I wound up to do what I've done a thousand times: throw the Frisbee the length of the field, which was about one hundred yards. This meant I was throwing it pretty hard. As I did, I heard a distinctive pop in my arm.

The next thing I knew, I was on the ground, writhing in intense pain. It was obvious I had torn something because the pain was excruciating. It was so bad that I couldn't sleep that night. At that point, I finally began to wonder if something was actually wrong with me—something muscular and minor, but something nonetheless. Worry really isn't a fifteen-year-old thing to do—not about little stuff like arm pain, at least.

However, whatever injury, twinge, or inflammation I was suffering from was now worse. I'd like to think that I didn't know my own strength, but let's be honest: it was a Frisbee—the lightest of all sports equipment. Even so, it hurt badly.

My mom again wanted me to go to the doctor, but I gave her a hard time about it. I was leaving for a leadership camp the next week, and I had no intention of letting anything mess up my big plans, especially in the prime of the summer. The camp wasn't the only thing on my immediate schedule, either. Upon my return, I was supposed to spend a week volunteering with my church youth group in the inner city of Indianapolis. Directly after that trip, I was slated to take another trip to King's Island.

Summer experiences were my business . . . and business was good.

More than Just a Strain

So, reluctantly, I let my parents ice my arm and put it in a sling. With my arm immobilized, the pain was more manageable, and I think I convinced myself (and more importantly, my parents) that it felt better. In retrospect, I doubt that it did; I just wasn't using it as much. Notwithstanding their reticence, I loaded up my things and set off to experience the various adventures before me and my friends. I was having the time of my life . . . living the high school dream.

With my arm secured in a sling, I was able to do all the things I wanted to do that summer: trekking through downtown Indy and then through the long lines leading up to roller coasters and attractions at King's Island. But before I left for this last trip, I had a conversation with my mom about my arm. She reluctantly let me go to King's Island, but she told me that no matter how late it might be when I got home, we were going to get my armed checked out early the next morning.

Even on those trips, my arm pain increased to the point that it affected my sleep. It was now clear that I couldn't avoid the doctor any longer. Mom followed through on her directive. The next morning after I came home, we went to a sports walk-in clinic for a quick X-ray so we could finally identify what was going on with my arm.

What I thought was going to be news about a muscle strain instead initiated mental and physical strain on me, my family, and my future . . . a strain that would never go away, not in this life anyway.

The doctor who read the X-ray at the clinic was obviously worried by what he saw on the films. He told my parents that there was a mass on my arm and that we needed to have an MRI done immediately. So we were off to another doctor for an MRI.

It's funny how doctors have to legally dance around teenagers, who are minors, in moments like these. I get it. They were doing their job and staying within the boundaries of HIPPA and whatnot. But during that sequence of events, a doctor never actually looked me in the eyes and said, "Tyler, you have cancer." But they did tell my parents—and I can't even imagine what those conversations must have felt like from their perspective.

Even though I did not yet know what the prognosis was, I could tell something wasn't right, if for no other reason than the way the doctors and nurses acted around me. It's not that they weren't extremely kind or personable. In some cases, it was that they were *too* kind and personable, almost to the point of concern. I was detecting the beginnings of sympathy, but I didn't know for what reason. The other telltale sign was that they kept wanting to run additional tests.

The doctor who read the MRI called my parents to officially confirm that what the medical team thought they might be seeing on the early scans was indeed there. Again, I had no idea at that point. My parents waited a little while and then called a family meeting. We sat down and read through a passage in the Bible together—Psalm 103. We talked about the fact that whatever we were going to have to face, we would face it together and always seek to honor God in it. They reminded me that God would be with us through whatever was to come. It was a reminder I would need to return to a million times in the years to come.

Then my poor heartbroken parents delivered to all of us the news that I had osteosarcoma—this thing called bone cancer.

CHAPTER 7

The New Abnormal Normal

(Tony & Kelly)

It was just a regular Thursday night. This was after Tyler had hurt his arm throwing a Frisbee but before we had taken him to have it scanned. He was wearing a sling to let the muscle strain heal. We had gathered at someone's house with a bunch of our friends, and all the kids were hanging out together in the backyard.

At one point, they all began walking back toward us up a hill. It was this moment when I (Kelly) remember thinking, *Something's wrong with Tyler.*

I just knew.

At fifteen, there are so many changes already going on inside the body. Baby fat finally goes away as growth spurts and other physical changes cause a host of scary yet exciting elements of the move into adulthood. But in that moment, I saw Tyler—I mean, I had always seen him, but my mother's intuition caused me to see him differently than I had in the past. He was thin—significantly thinner than he had been only a few months before.

Up to that point, the pulled muscle in his arm just seemed like one of those things that just randomly happens to rambunctious boys when they work out too hard or run into each other on the basketball court. But in this moment, I knew we needed to get him to a doctor and get it looked at.

I can't say that I panicked. I certainly didn't think it was cancer. I just knew that something felt off. I never verbalized anything of the sort—after all, saying it out loud would make it a little too real. But deep down inside, I knew something peculiar was going on.

"Well, that's not good."

Tyler told me that he overheard these words from the X-ray tech at the Methodist Sports Clinic here in Carmel. She obviously meant nothing by it except that the X-ray seemed anomalous—that is, not what she was expecting. Of course, my first thought was, *I hope that didn't worry Tyler.* That's where I still was—right where any "normal" mother would be: trying to protect our son from undue anxiousness.

But worry was about to be the least of my concerns.

I didn't have much time to worry about it myself as the doctor was quickly with us in the room. "No. No," said the doctor examining the X-ray. "See this right here? This should not be here. This should not be here."

I'm not sure how many times he actually said it, but it felt like a hundred. "This should not be here."

Then he added, "We need an MRI, stat."

We had some trouble with our insurance company getting the MRI covered. As I was trying to work it out, the nurse from the clinic called and said the doctor didn't care about insurance; he wanted me to bring Tyler in for the MRI right away and deal with insurance later. So I took him in and let them perform the MRI and then headed toward our house, which was only about a ten-minute drive. But only five minutes passed before the doctor called my phone.

"Mrs. Trent, while I'm not an oncologist, and I can't be 100 percent certain, I am pretty convinced that your son has Ewing sarcoma." That was the phone call that changed our lives.

That was the moment we all got cancer.

One of Tyler's friends had ridden along with us to the MRI, so thankfully, the kids were in the backseat talking to each other as the doctor filled my ear with the frightening next steps about which doctors we needed to go see immediately and so forth. I really don't remember everything the doctor said—I was shell-shocked. I pulled into the driveway, and the kids got out of the car and went inside. I stayed in the car and called Tony.

$$T^2$$

I (Tony) will never forget the call that afternoon. It's similar to the way that everyone seems to remember where they were and what they were doing on September 11 when the planes crashed into the twin towers. I was on my way home, driving on I-465—the loop that circles Indianapolis—when the phone buzzed.

"Something is seriously wrong with Tyler," Kelly said on the other end. We couldn't finish talking then, but I was not far from home, so I speeded up to get there quickly.

When I pulled up, she was still in the driveway. We both got out of our cars. I'll never forget the look on her face when she told me the news. Her face was beyond pale, almost colorless. I could see the streaks on her cheeks where the tears had already found their path. My stomach knotted up—this was going to be something bad. She could barely look at me when she faintly uttered the word no one ever wants to hear.

Cancer.

$$T^2$$

I (Kelly) could barely get the word out before Tony began crying. We collapsed into each other's arms. My first thought was actually a million thoughts all crammed into one: *Will he make it? Will we be able to beat this? What is he going to have to go through? What about our other kids? How is this going to affect all of us?*

We were a very healthy family—how could this happen? We constantly engaged in outdoor activities and exercise, so how could one of us be this sick and not know it? It was like I was watching someone else walking around in a fog. It certainly couldn't be us.

We didn't tell Tyler immediately. We just couldn't do it yet, so we let him have one more Friday night as a "normal" teenager. It was the last one of his life. The next morning, instead of having Saturday waffles, we called all our kids together to tell them something we couldn't believe we were about to say.

First, Tony read Psalm 103 to the whole family and told them that no matter what was ahead, we were going to try to honor God through the good or bad. We never dreamed what all this would look like in the days and years to come.

Then he broke the news to them—that our oldest son and the brother they all looked up to the most—had cancer.

I honestly don't remember everything Tony said—only that he did most of the talking. All I could do was cry. The boys were devastated and each scattered to his own room—they were all weeping. Tyler lay on his face in his closet crying, sometimes pounding his fist on the floor out of fear and frustration. I went from room to room trying to comfort each of my sons the best that I could.

I (Tony) wandered through the hallway in a fog, not knowing what to do. I just kept crying out to God, trying to find and take comfort in whatever scriptures I could recall at the time, including Psalm 23. I begged God to be our shepherd right then, right there. This was one of the hardest moments we would ever know.

CHAPTER 8

Brokenness

(Tyler)

People have often asked me about my very first thoughts when I heard the news that I had cancer. That's a pretty tough question because I think my head was filled with about a billion different thoughts. Even so, I definitely have a profound memory in that moment—an impression, if you will, about a specific scripture. 1 Thessalonians 5:16–18 is a verse about gratitude, prayer, and a divine will that I still don't fully understand. This scripture became one of the foundational elements that have defined so much of my story since the very first moment that cancer became my reality.

Anchors

I believe there are moments in life when God drops something into your mind or heart that acts like an anchor. An anchor is something that is so heavy and strong that it can be securely tied off to when currents or storms threaten to send a ship off course, or worse, send it to the bottom of the ocean. Historically, a sailor would never take a trip without an anchor because he knew beyond the shadow of a doubt that there would be moments when he would need the anchor to avoid getting lost or running aground.

For me, 1 Thessalonians 5:16–18 has been that anchor. It says, "Rejoice always; pray without ceasing; in everything give thanks; for this is God's will for you in Christ Jesus" (NIV). It feels like an anchor that I didn't choose—one that God chose for me.

It is hard for me to separate this verse—and the role my faith has played in my journey—from the details of my story or how I felt when I first learned of my diagnosis. So when I say this was an anchor, it feels almost literal. It was a huge deal for me. It didn't make me perfect or keep me from ever coming apart at the seams. I did come unraveled, but I found that Christ never left me—he kept weaving me back together, even when I questioned him.

The fact that we associate faith with brokenness proves just how broken our view of faith really is. This saddens me. All too often, we keep some unnecessary distance from God because we have heard—or just develop the impression—that he wants us to keep such a distance, at least until we get our lives cleaned up a bit.

We tend to think of God as an anchor that holds us back rather than one that holds us steady. The shocking truth is that such a way of thinking is the complete opposite of Christ's message—that he was born, died, and rose from the dead—to deliver to people just like you and me. He is not distant from our most broken places; rather, he has come near them. He is near us when we feel far away from him. He is not waiting on us to move; he has already moved toward us.

We can't get to him; he comes to us instead. He doesn't require transformation; he offers it . . . and even paid for it with his own life. So when I say I'm a man of faith, I want you to know what I mean. I don't mean that I'm not broken just as much or more than everyone else, only that I try to keep entrusting my brokenness to Christ. Instead of spending this life trying to repair myself or clean myself up, I rely on Jesus to do these things in me instead.

I didn't know in that first moment of learning that I had cancer just how much I would need this anchor. His love, acceptance, and comforting nearness have been the only things that have kept me from just giving up. Well, to be honest, a few times I have tried to give up, but even then, Jesus pursued me in a thousand different ways, including the daily patience of my family, the constant support of my friends, and the extraordinary kindness of strangers. I have experienced his anchor in moments of prayer—sometimes quiet and comforting and sometimes gut-wrenching and demanding.

At every turn, the real grace of Jesus for me—and for you—has only required that I keep showing up with my brokenness. When I do, he has promised that he will already be there waiting. Before I was ever a Christ-follower, Christ was a Tyler-chaser.

So when I found out I had cancer, Jesus was already there ahead of me with grace, comforting me. Of course, there were a million parallel thoughts in my mind as well, a million reasons to freak out. Please don't think that I was only thinking spiritual thoughts in this dark moment, because I was not.

In fact, I remember my first practical concern being whether or not I was going to lose my arm. In the early hours of the revelation, especially being a teenager, I did not fully understand what osteosarcoma really was. Those were the early stages of my involuntary education.

All I knew was that there was a tumor on my arm and that it was eating away at my bone. More importantly, I knew that if they didn't remove it—and fast—it was going to kill me. It's hard to communicate the shock that came in that moment, the escalation of emotions from thinking the day before that I possibly had a serious muscle tear that would affect my skills on the basketball court and at Ultimate Frisbee to seeing the potential of my whole future being torn from me.

It was also the last moment I remember as "childhood."

What Is Cancer?

What is cancer? You probably know what it technically is, but for anyone who has faced it for himself or herself—or alongside a family member or friend—you know that its devastating effects are so much more than merely technical or medical. Though there are many known causes, as well as much confusion about what causes it, some believe that cancer is a disease that every human has in his or her body in some form or fashion. It's just a matter of whether or not our immune systems are able to fight it off on a day-to-day basis. Most healthy human beings are able to do that.

Unfortunately, I am apparently not one of these healthy human beings.

Regardless—and I hate to give cancer too much of my time—it is a terrible disease that wrecks pretty much everything around it, including family, friendships, hopes, and dreams. It was nothing short of devastating to learn about my diagnosis. It came out of left field—after all, most teenagers are worrying about driver's licenses and prom dates, not whether or not they will survive long enough to see college.

This diagnosis began rapidly chipping away at my naïveté, but there was still so much I didn't know at first. Sure, I knew it was bad, but in my family, the only person close to me up to that point who had ever had cancer was my grandfather—my dad's dad. His cancer was supposedly a result of smoking his entire life. He eventually developed lung cancer, but went into remission years before my first diagnosis. I don't think his journey through treatment had ever registered with me.

So most of the information about cancer I possessed at the time was made up of tidbits I had picked up from the news or social media. These stories somehow don't seem as real when you read about them among the hundreds of posts that scroll each day down your social media feed.

I knew cancer was happening in other people's lives and families, but I had little context to understand what they were really going through. That absence of context began changing rapidly. Tragically. As I learned more and more about cancer, my mind gravitated toward catastrophe rather than hope.

I'm going to lose my arm.

I'm going to die.

I'm never going to make it to college.

I'm never going to get married.

Emotionally, I dove headlong into the worst of the worst-case scenarios, and it sent me to a very dark place, for sure.

The tumor was on my humerus. The pain I had been feeling for months had now become unyielding . . . it never stopped. As we began to explore the path ahead, we learned that the standard method for treating osteosarcoma in the United States basically involved amputation, followed by an intense regimen of chemotherapy. They wanted me to go into the hospital every week for four days of chemotherapy. Every once in a while, I would get a week off. Thankfully, they did not want to amputate my arm, but the surgery was still going to be complicated because of the extensive damage.

We didn't realize it until after I had the surgery, but when I had thrown that Frisbee, I had broken my arm. That's how weak my bone had become from the tumor eating away at it. The surgeons had to spend an extra two hours in the operating room picking bone fragments out of my muscle because my bone had shattered. They said my bone was like a cracked, spider-webbed window that someone had thrown a baseball at.

Let that sink in: the only thing holding my arm together was the tumor itself.

There's no sugarcoating how I felt during that year: it was pure hell. I've been told that some of the most painful things humans can endure are giving birth, passing kidney stones, and having osteosarcoma. After that moment of the infamous Frisbee toss, I lived in constant, unrelenting pain.

Our Issues with the Refs

People often ask me where I have found the strength to keep going. I have survived emotionally for one reason alone: Christ. I can't tell you any one way that it works, but I can tell you with complete honesty that Jesus keeps providing me with the strength and the peace I have every day because I know that God enters into my suffering.

From the beginning, he planned the ultimate upset. The world is full of suffering, and I have experienced my own share of it. But the real message of God's plan for this world is not just about a baby born in a stable, nor is it just about a savior who went to a cross for us. It began long, long before that. When humankind invited suffering into this world, God had already planned a way to someday make all things right.

It's not just rhetoric to help us deal with the ill effects of living in all this pain and brokenness. For many, it seems too easy an answer just to trust that someone else is working on the problem and is trustworthy to make sure it all makes sense in the end. But you have to ask yourself: Does the opposite—a life devoid of any sort of divine design, purpose, or trust—solve the grand issues and mysteries of pain, suffering, and the search for meaning in this life?

I have been down those roads as well, and while there are many valid questions that we can and should ask, I never found more meaning in faithless answers than I have found in trusting in a personal, knowable, gracious Father who is stronger, smarter, and higher than me.

The issue is whether or not he is truly trustworthy . . . *this* is the real crux of the issue.

If you think God's job is to make sure everything works out great every day of your life, then you will be disappointed in him—not disappointed in the real God, but in a culturally contrived version of him. Take the word of a dying man: God does incredible miracles in normal people's lives every day. He is a healer. He is immeasurably good.

He does grant wishes, but he is not a genie.

I get it. Many people can't bring themselves to trust God and the mysteriously divine strategy he has been mapping out since before we were even tiny dots on the map of history and eternity, because they think he has promised something that he hasn't—to keep our lives free of trouble and suffering.

He has promised the exact opposite: "I have told you these things, so that in me you may have peace. In this world *you will have trouble.* But take heart! I have overcome the world" (John 14:33, NIV, emphasis mine).

In this world, we will have trouble. It is a fact—a temporary fact, but a fact nonetheless. Someday, the trouble of this season, of this world, will pass into the reality of the next season, and the trouble we face here will cease. When that day comes, there will be no more of this daily struggle against temptation, depression, and anxiety. No child will ever have to be told that she has cancer and might not live to see her eighteenth birthday. It is coming.

But he has not yet come.

Why is he delaying? Why does he let us face all this trouble? Why does he let *me* face this cancer? Well, I don't have all the answers here, but I do have a few thoughts; the difficulty of my situation has forced me to think about these types of things. As hard as it is to believe, even his delay in ending these troubles is a reflection of his deep and abiding grace for us. " The Lord is not slow to fulfill his promise as some count slowness, but is patient toward you, not wishing that any should perish, but that all should reach repentance" (2 Peter 3:9, ESV).

I think we often think of God as if he is a referee out on the field of life. From the grandstands of daily living, we are pretty far from the field, yet we are still attentive to the game. Offense. Defense. Special plays. We are mesmerized, watching every move. Good days make us cheer. Bad days make us boo. And often, we complain about the calls we think are wrong. "What are you, blind? How could you call that!"

Now, I don't know about you, but I've *never* yelled at the refs. (I'm not sure if my sarcasm will bleed through the page, but here's hoping.) We all do it. Those who sit in the "student section" may have a little better vantage point of the field. These spectators are like the people who dive deep into the mysteries of God through study and discipline. But they are still not standing where the referee is.

As we all know, it is often the fans sitting in the student section who are the most ravenous and unreasonable in their objections about the call made out on the field, despite the fact that they often have a better view of the game than the other people in the stands. In the same way, sometimes the very religion that should allow us to better trust the referee instead causes us to begin caring more about the collective desire of the masses around us (our fellow fans, or fellow religious people) than the real call—the one that is not supposed to be ours, but God's.

Most of us are sitting somewhere in the stadium just trying to follow the game. And from the cheap seats of trying to survive your work day, your family complexities, and perhaps a very real crisis of health, faith, or relationship, the game can start looking pretty far away and difficult to understand.

But the referee? He has the best seat in the house, so to speak.

His is a bird's-eye view, not a view from the cheap seats of humanity. What appears to be out of bounds from fifty-seven rows up may actually be in bounds to the one person who is standing six inches from the play. But we argue. We scream. We shake our fists at the ref (God), wondering why he is so blind.

The irony is, we are the ones who are really blind. It is our distance from the purest viewpoint of reality, purpose, and eternity that keeps us from seeing. Even so, in sports, most of modern culture never agrees with the ref *if* the call is not a call they want.

It's a trust issue—no one trusts the ref.

I'm right up here in the stands with you. When I first heard that I had cancer, I was furious with the referee of life. I felt that I couldn't trust him.

I would come to find out that he is actually the only one I can fully trust, and this drastic transformation is the real reason you are reading these words. It didn't happen overnight, and it was far from easy, but as you will see, it *did* happen.

If it can happen to me, then I am convinced it can happen to you, too.

CHAPTER 9

The Worse Before the Better

(Tyler)

As a sports writer, I am familiar with the idea that big changes—even ones that will eventually lead to a seemingly better trajectory for a team or athletic department—sometimes bring along with them an initial turbulent state of difficulty and uncertainty. Change of any kind is rarely easy, which is why we are prone to settle into familiar places and hunker down, even if these may not be the best places to be.

When it comes to college football specifically, a coaching change can create mixed results in the beginning of the process. Division 1 college football programs are generally the behemoths of post-secondary athletics, boasting huge rosters, huge facilities, huge profits, and huge coaching staffs. Unlike many other collegiate sports that have smaller rosters and require a staff of fewer than ten coaches, a D-1 football team necessitates a small army of coaches, strength and conditioning personnel, analysts, and support staff. And of course, when they all move to town, their spouses and children come with them. It is as if a small city disappears and another is transplanted in its place overnight.

So when there is a coaching change, it is a major ordeal. The entire culture of a program begins to shift—and just like shifting tectonic plates, a changing program can cause earthquake-sized tremors that shake things up for everyone involved. New leadership philosophies. New disciplinary policies. New communication methods. New offensive plays. New defensive schemes. During such a transition period, from what was once familiar to something that is so very new, everything can feel off, even though everything may be on the path to becoming better than it was before.

As they say, sometimes things get worse before they get better.

The Scary New

That is a pretty accurate reflection of what I went through in the immediate aftermath of being diagnosed with cancer. For the first several months, things got a lot worse before they had a chance to get better. I was still in pain, so that was obviously where my disappointment began. But there was so much more affecting me than just physical discomfort. I felt like my innermost self was unraveling.

Again, there was the tortuous speculation about the endless possibilities of everything I could lose in this life. Dear-to-my-heart things that seemed to be just within my reach only a day earlier now seemed a million miles away. Would I ever even get to walk across a high school graduation stage, much less a college platform? Would I ever have a wife? Or a kid? There was so much to process. It was like an enormous dump truck of change ran me over, then backed up to where I was lying and continued to unload more change on me.

I felt buried and forgotten.

I was thrust into learning a whole new culture and language—the cancer-ridden life. All the medical terms. A new schedule that was no longer centered around an exciting upcoming trip with school or friends. No more random moments to just hang out with friends for no other reason than the fun of doing so. No more trivial moments of adolescence that are like glue holding together the cracks of all the excitement and fear that come along with being almost adults—the emotional adrenaline rush of all that could be in the future. It is not just the intentional moments, but also the trivial ones that make life fun, and now life felt so serious and overwhelming.

People often talk about the difficulty that comes along with the *fear of the unknown.* I certainly felt that fear. But in many ways, cancer also robbed me of *the joy of the unknown.* Instead of spending time speculating and dreaming with my friends and family about a hundred different future paths that all seemed pretty feasible at the age of fifteen, I was thinking about cancer.

Only cancer.

Cancer has robbed me of many things, but this one—this joy of the unknown, something I'm not even sure most people realize they possess since it is so often eclipsed by their corresponding fear of the unknown—was a loss I immediately felt in the depths of my young heart. I now completely knew what was next for me in life, or at least for the next nine months. The battle against cancer was going to dominate my time, energy, and thinking—not just for me, but also for my family.

I was about to be forced to ingest more strong medications than most people ever will. However, the loss of the joy of the unknown was one of the toughest pills to swallow.

What would the first needle—the portal of my first chemo treatment—feel like when it pierced my skin and entered my vein? What would the medicine feel like coursing through my body? How would I respond to the treatment? All the unknowns ahead of me were devoid of joy.

I was a fairly astute fifteen-year-old, but now I had to grow leaps and bounds in my education about what chemotherapy really is: low doses of poison designed to kill the cells within your body, administered with the intent of doing just that. The hope is that cancer cells won't survive the chemical onslaught but that your healthy cells will. Chemotherapy is like setting off a tear-gas grenade in your own house to attempt to stop a violent intruder . . . while you're still in it. Even if it works, you're going to feel the same effects that the invader feels.

I began to get a clearer picture of what was ahead—I was going to have to harm myself to harm my cancer. That terrified me. I was right to be scared because cancer really sucks.

Just as there is *fear of the unknown* and *joy of the unknown,* there is also *fear of the known,* which I was now feeling, and *joy of the known,* which was nowhere to be found. It felt like the cancer was literally killing my joy. Everything ahead looked scary and dark, even though I had no choice but to walk through it.

If I wanted any hope of a better place beyond the pain and instability ahead of me, I had no other option but to point my compass directly toward that very pain and instability. I was moving toward a treatment ultimately aimed at the goal of saving my life, but the ground beneath my feet felt steep and slippery.

The Premath and the Aftermath

Even though I was still a kid, I was already a statistician at heart. Even when I was younger, I rarely watched a game without knowing the corresponding stats beforehand. The quarterback's season completion percentage. Receivers' rates of dropped passes. Yards after contact. Missed tackles. Third-down conversion rates. Expert journalists, which I aspired to be, know that these numbers are more than just nerdy musings of sports enthusiasts. They help coaches and players prepare to face their opponents with precision, intentionality, and strategy.

What respected coach would enter a game without watching film on the opponent?

I am wired to seek out data, so cancer was no different. I began learning all about osteosarcoma. I learned that I faced some very steep odds. Osteosarcoma cells that are localized—that is, still residing in the area where they originated—generally equate to a five-year survival rate of about 60 to 80 percent. I was discouraged just by the fact that such a thing as a "five-year survival rate" even existed. I wanted a cure.

But the more information I gathered, the bleaker it looked—if the cancer were to spread to other parts of the body outside the origination point, the five-year survival rate descended to only about 15 to 30 percent. This alarming statistic clearly meant that my treatment path—and my need to get started on it as soon as possible—were incredibly important factors. This treatment path became my new known—a necessary evil. After all, when there is nothing but an aggressively growing tumor holding your arm together, you can't logically leave it there and just hope for the best.

The treatment path looked like this: nine months of chemotherapy with a complete replacement of my humerus about halfway through. Nine months is the time it takes for a new life to be born; I was hoping I would also have a new life in nine months.

Chemotherapy sucks. Going into your arm, the needle just feels like any other IV, but the aftermath is unlike anything you've ever felt. Some people talk about feeling various sensations while they are actually undergoing the treatment, such as warmness, coolness, or itchiness. At times, I felt a little bit of everything.

There are a lot of different side effects, some of which I was blessed not to experience or experience very often, but many that I did. They included nausea coupled with a general loss of appetite. You would think that as you are wearing down your body to kill the cancer cells, your body would crave nourishment to build itself back up, but this was not always the case.

One of the most significant issues I faced during chemotherapy was what people sometimes call "chemo brain." The physical toll doesn't just stop with your body; chemo has physiological side effects, meaning it affects both your body and your brain. The result is a general fogginess of mind. Trains of thought stop running on time . . . and sometimes they don't arrive at their stations at all.

The result is that your mind needs more time to process questions and produce coherent thoughts and words. It becomes difficult to think things through—things that you previously could process in merely a few seconds. Attentiveness becomes a real challenge.

Did I mention that chemotherapy sucks?

So does osteosarcoma. There was no genetic reason behind my diagnosis. Nothing that I ate or was exposed to. No marker that anyone knows of. It just happened. Dwelling on the "whys" of my diagnosis is a walk down a path that doesn't end at a healthy mental place. Even so, there have been times I have laced up my boots and tried.

It was this process of trying to understand and ultimately *beat* cancer that actually *beat* me down the most.

During those first four months of chemo, I hit a really dark place. I sank deep into depression, so deep that I almost never emerged from it. I blame some of it on being fifteen years old and still immature. I don't call myself immature to be hard on my younger self. It was just the way I was. Who at such a tender age could go through such a horrible experience and not find themselves at the bottom of a deep emotional and spiritual hole?

But immaturity was only the first ingredient; there were many more. Fear. Pain. Anxiety. And of course, the altered state of thinking that came along with the chemotherapy. I have come to accept that this last ingredient probably played a larger role than I originally gave it credit for—or better stated, blame.

Depression is a complex thing that can't be summed up easily. I think we want to make things simpler than they are because we want to find the quickest path to "fixing" the problem. If you have a flat tire, the task ahead is simple and direct: get a new tire or repair the old one. But when it comes to the mind, there is generally no such thing as a simple or direct path to "repair."

So I really can't fully know what was happening in my brain during that time. The thing about having millions of synapses is that if one or two of them get tangled or crossed, it's difficult to know where to begin trying to unravel the mess. It's not as simple as untying a knot in your shoestring.

But beyond the countless variables swirling about in the medical and physiological components of my depression that I cannot identify, I *can* identify what I was thinking at the time. For me, it was an intense time of questioning God. I imagine that most people question God when they are diagnosed with cancer because it is such a seemingly random and utterly senseless diagnosis. Having never seen it coming, it hit me squarely in the heart—and my heart struggled with that which was most important to it: my trust in Christ. God just didn't seem trustworthy anymore.

When I learned that the most common first step in the treatment for osteosarcoma in the United States was amputation, just the idea of losing my right arm caused me to lose confidence deep down in my soul. There was also a loss of my identity as someone who considered himself to be a reliable leader. I usually made the best grades. I was the first one to lead and the first one for a teacher at our co-op to ask to help another student, even if only by just talking with him or her through a difficult personal situation. So when this crisis hit and I had to stop attending our co-op for a time, it felt like I was suddenly losing not only my life, but also so many of the things that made my life worth living. It felt like the cancer was now my identity. That I was no longer a leader . . . no longer Tyler.

Overwhelmed with so much loss in this new normal, I fell apart.

Again, who knows what all the variables were, but the result was clear—at some point, I decided I was going to kill myself. I know that the idea of killing yourself because you're upset that something else might kill you sounds counterintuitive, but it was so real to me. We tend to think that the most primal instinct within the human psyche is the drive to survive at all costs. But during my terrified, altered state of looking at the world through a lens of pain, hopelessness, and worry, I think that this seemingly most basic of instincts morphed into something else altogether: the desperation to find relief.

I'm no psychologist, but I imagine that this is where many people dealing with extreme physical and mental illnesses also arrive. It is a scary place to care more about resolution than survival because of the pain and fear weighing you down, promising to continue to torment you at every turn in the foreseeable future.

I wish I could have been stronger. I wish I could have endured the fear and the pain with more grace and courage. I wish I could have been the inspirational figure *then* that so many loving people around the country have made me out to be *now*. But I simply was not. I was weak. I was beaten down. I was scared.

I wasn't sure that living *through* this was worth the possibility of living at all.

At my lowest point, I actually did try to take my own life. I decided that either cancer was going to kill me, or I was going to do it. I attempted to do so several times, but was obviously unsuccessful. It doesn't really matter how I tried; it only matters that I tried.

Since I have experienced some of these dark moments, my heart for others who feel this low has grown exponentially. It is not a club that I ever wanted to be a part of, but I am a part of it nonetheless . . . and I empathize with all those who also call themselves members.

If you're not a part of this club and you know someone who is, or if you are worried at all someone you know may be considering suicide, it is easy to get stuck in the frustration over the fact that they might be willing to consider such a thing at all. It is easy to be upset with them. Dealing with someone you care about who is suicidal is a painful thing, and it can make you feel that the other person is being selfish.

Can't they see the huge aftershocks that their momentary act would cause? Guilt. Grief. Financial constraints. Depression. Lack of a parent or a son or a daughter. I can't speak definitively about each of these, but I can tell you that there is much validity to family and friends feeling these emotions toward those for whom they care who also happen to be nearing the edge of suicidal and self-harming actions.

But as one who has been to the brink and has come back to tell about it, I can assure you that when your most basic instinct has somehow shifted from survival to relief, there is an overwhelming state of mind that tries to take over your consciousness, displacing (or at least temporarily disabling) your innate desire to avoid being selfish or flippant toward your loved ones. In these cloudy moments, you can't see straight, so you also can't walk straight. In fact, it is actually very common for people to somehow fiercely believe and insist that everyone in their lives would be better off without them, no matter how many times they are told this is not true.

When your ears are clogged with pain and fear, it's hard to hear the truth.

I am so grateful that I did not succeed here. However, the fact that I tried did change a few things. Yes, I eventually regained my better senses, along with my will to live. Even so, since that experience, I asked my family to implement a few precautions simply because I now know that I can't trust myself . . . I need God and others. This means that they made sure I had limited access to medicines that could be dangerous in high doses. I also asked them to make sure there were never any sharp objects left lying around me.

To this day, I don't even carry a pocket knife because of this experience.

Hurting People

I may not carry a knife of any size, but I still cut some people. It wasn't just my body that I attempted to kill—it was also some of my relationships. I still have a lot of remorse and regret for the people I hurt during that time.

Our homeschool co-op was very close-knit. We shared life together not just as friends, but also as families. Everyone knew everyone else, and everyone knew everyone else's business—good, bad, and ugly.

Well, my "business" during that time went from bad to ugly.

My mind-set at the time was detrimental to my relationships. My words and reactions became very sharp. My patience was greatly affected by the depression and by the chemo, so I began to butt heads with everyone around me.

The thing is, I really don't like ongoing or unresolved conflict. So why did I become so contentious? Well, it became easier to try to end the tension by just saying something crazy or offensive that would ruin the relationship. Closing doors was easier than trying to walk through them. Out of the loneliness of my situation, I actively pushed people away.

It was as if my relational instincts changed to the point that keeping those once-crucial connections alive and healthy was simply no longer as high a priority as it once was. Just like my physical condition, I wanted relief. And I thought I had to find that relief alone because I felt utterly alone in the situation.

I also had an innate feeling that people were somehow wronging me. Who knows where that came from, but again, there were so many things spinning in my orbit that it was easy to feel sick from all the dizzying motion. Perhaps I had a subconscious envy toward each of them who still possessed the joy of the unknown I had lost. Perhaps I illogically felt that they were a part of some grand, divine conspiracy that had brought me to this place.

When *everything* feels like an attack, *everyone* can feel like an enemy.

I didn't understand what I was feeling, so I didn't understand how to control my words. Even so, I don't think I ever anticipated that people would react negatively toward me when I acted negatively toward them. I had a strange sense of tragic narcissism. Even though I hated it, it felt like everything revolved around me—or more accurately, my cancer.

Everyone was still moving ahead with their lives. Everyone was not, in fact, revolving around my cancer. Even though I wanted to hurt my friends because I had become disillusioned with them, I still somehow felt justifiably hurt when they reacted to my hurtfulness.

Yes, you would think I would have understood, but I didn't. And though I try to avoid clichés, sometimes something is a common saying because it is actually true, as is the case with this expression: "Hurting people hurt people."

I was so surprised that they didn't understand, even though I didn't understand, either. They were just kids, too, so they couldn't understand my situation any more than I could. The changes in my life were scary for them, too, which irritated me because no one else was having to live the nightmare but me. In my mind, they shouldn't have had the right to be afraid when I was the one who was actually suffering from this disease. Somehow even the sympathy of others felt isolating to me, to the point that I rejected it.

I know I acted harshly toward my family during that time as well, but I think I put them into a different mental category than other people simply because of their daily proximity. They were with me constantly, so they were the only people who could help make me feel that I wasn't completely alone, even though I knew they couldn't fully understand what I was feeling. I suppose the mind seeks solid ground, even when you don't tell it to.

My family was the only solid ground I knew—and I can't imagine how hard this season of my life was on them.

I think people don't often consider the way the treatment process itself can be physically isolating. It can lead to deeper depression and emotional isolation. During chemo treatments, your body can become immunocompromised, so you have to try to avoid certain situations where germs can be easily transferred or shared.

If a friend has a cold and wants to visit, there's a good chance he or she will have to stay away because of the possibility of causing a life-threatening secondary health crisis for the patient. But this also creates a secondary emotional crisis because of the isolation and lack of contact. It is complex on every level.

Regardless, my attempt to drive away many friends during this time was not completely successful. Some of them looked past my thorny attitude and kept coming back for more. These friends are forever in my heart—people like Josh Seals, Jake Heinzman, Anni Osborne, Noah Osborne, and several others. Like the love of my family, the love of my friends overwhelmed me—and still does.

CHAPTER 10

Devils . . . Red and Otherwise

(Tony & Kelly)

C ancer hit our son like a ton of bricks—and for a while, it seemed to crush his very identity, leaving no trace of the boy we once knew. Tyler was an exceptional child who had grown into an exceptional teenager. He was persistent, responsible, and driven. But he was also well balanced and good-natured. Easy to get along with. Always cracking a joke. Always having lots of friends.

Without even trying, Tyler was a leader. He was always out front, helping and leading throughout middle school and high school. It seemed so natural to him—just an extension of his personality and character. And just as naturally as he would lead, people also seemed to naturally want to follow him.

He was also an incredible student, taking his studies seriously. The thing about Tyler as a homeschooler was that he pretty much taught himself. His big joke was that when the time came to start thinking about colleges for Blake, Tyler was going to have to help us with all the applications—because he did it all for himself. We went on several college visits, and he arranged all of them, telling us where to be and when to be there. I think all I did was fill out the Free Application for Federal Student Aid (FASFA).

But before we could ever take our eighteen-year-old on college visits, we found ourselves on a ride with the fifteen-year-old version of him who was just trying to survive. The emotional pain was overbearing. To see our son lose all his strength. To witness his loss of identity as a student, leader, and friend. To watch our other children also carry the weight of cancer. The bottom line is that parents should never have to tell their child that he or she has cancer, which is why we are working so hard to help researchers find a cure.

So much of Tyler's struggle was a result of undergoing chemotherapy. His regimen consisted of a combination of three drugs: Methotrexate, Cisplatin, and Doxorubicin. These drugs have been around a long time, and if you read about their side effects, you would never even think about taking them voluntarily. It's basically like taking rat poison—with cancer being the rat, if a rat were living inside you.

Doxorubicin is often nicknamed "The Red Devil" or "Red Death" because of its deep red color and dangerous side effects. We were fortunate that Tyler didn't experience a lot of the nausea many patients have. The most devastating effects were more emotional in nature.

Tyler seemed to face an extra-hard struggle here because he seemed to personally feel that he should be able to fight these emotional side effects better than he actually could. He was always pretty hard on himself about the way he acted during that time. Although we are proud that he always took responsibility for himself, the truth is that these drugs temporarily altered his personality in ways that he could not prevent with intellect or willpower.

It was a daily fight to find joy. Even the scripture that had first inspired him to give thanks at all times, along with many supportive people constantly encouraging him by calling him "Tyler Strong," just seemed to somehow make him feel worse—like he was somehow a fake. He knew he was not thankful and not strong—and these realities tortured his mind as much as the drugs tortured his body.

He simply wanted to die. These were the days that threatened to do us in as parents—watching our son lose the will to live. There were times that we found him hiding in his closet, just trying to get away from everything he couldn't hide from. His sixteenth birthday party was an absolute disaster that left him crying by himself, away from his friends, for most of the day. At one point, I (Kelly) had to sleep on his bedroom floor next to him for many nights on end, just to make sure he didn't hurt himself, or worse.

As he fell apart, we scurried about trying to catch the pieces and put him back together. Our boy whose nickname in school was Smiley had gone from a happy-go-lucky kid to a suicidal cancer patient—and watching him become so broken broke us in ways from which we may never fully recover on this side of heaven. We were not only losing our physical child to sickness; we were also losing his personality and temperament . . . the person we knew God made him to be.

Tyler's crisis was multifaceted, but a huge part of it stemmed from the fact that he lost his identity as a leader among his fellow homeschoolers. God gifted Tyler to lead, and everyone in his class followed him; in fact, everyone around Tyler seemed to look up to him. He was often chosen to help with younger students and those who needed a little extra encouragement. Sure, he made mistakes like any kid does, but he had an unusual strength in the areas of leadership and expressiveness.

This was just as true with adults as it was with kids. Teachers used to say things like, "I don't know what God's going to do with Tyler, but I can't wait to see what his journey is going to be because he's made for big things." A teacher who had Tyler as a student when he was only eight years old wrote to tell us that back then, she had just moved to Indy, didn't know anyone yet, and was going through a really hard time in her life. She said she looked forward to seeing Tyler because he would always go out of his way to say hello and put a smile on her face. He was an eight-year-old encouraging a grown woman.

One of his teachers he had later in high school, Ashley Morgan, later wrote to us about Tyler:

> *Tyler was more than a charismatic cancer hero—he was my student. He was the clever, incredibly intelligent, friendly, persuasive, hilarious, and down-to-earth eighteen-year-old whose writing made me laugh and made me think. Knowing Tyler, I always felt like I was on the periphery of something bigger. It was a strange feeling, and I couldn't have explained it at that time. I'm not sure I can explain it now. I felt like I*

was witnessing something. He felt somehow larger than life. Not because he was loud or had a large presence (he didn't). It was a subtle feeling that I was seeing a small part of something important play out. Something that would be bigger than our classroom. It was a humbling feeling: the same feeling I have now because we know that something bigger is going on. Something bigger than even Tyler.

Ashley was describing our son, but during that season of his life, he was somebody else altogether. It felt like we lost him for a time—and it kind of felt like we lost ourselves, too, in the madness of trying to keep up with it all.

You don't always realize in the moment the blessing it is to be able to simply sit down as a family and eat dinner together. Our family was completely scattered during this season. One of us (usually Kelly) was always either living in Tyler's room or living with him in the hospital. It would be two weeks at one place and then two or three at the other. Rinse and repeat. We lived uprooted.

Our family had always been very active, but vacations and activities—even holiday traditions—all either changed completely or came to a screeching halt. At times, both of our younger sons were living at other places with family or friends, simply because of our logistical and medical challenges with Tyler. We know they both felt invisible at times, supporting their brother and understanding his situation, but also feeling that their lives were on hold as so much of the family's energy was being consumed with keeping Tyler alive. Tyler was always getting visitors, gifts, and their parents' attention. We were doing the best we could, and so were his siblings, but it broke our hearts that there was no way everyone could receive all the attention they deserved.

We just had to survive, but it didn't feel like we were living. And of course, all this was costing a ridiculous amount of money. I (Tony) was still trying to run my business, sprinting from work to the hospital and trying to keep up with everything that was going on while also not abandoning my wife and our other two sons.

We started this journey through cancer with a spiritual perspective, and we clung to our faith throughout the entire ordeal. But we want people who are struggling with cancer, or who know someone who is, to realize that this is still such a difficult path. We were so very thankful for Tyler's youth group, who really supported him. One night, a bunch of the students and leaders shaved their heads. His youth pastor, Joe Wittmer, and the other youth leaders and friends were amazing. They spent a lot of time with him at the hospital and at our home on a regular basis, playing board games with him and trying to help him feel like himself.

But as much as they wanted to be helpful, his friends were still living their lives, as they should have been. This was so hard because his life was, at best, on hold—and at worst, it was in serious jeopardy. So many things were happening at school and at church that he would have been leading or at least involved in with his friends, but he just couldn't. He was missing out on life, which, combined with the chemo and pain, left him crying a lot, often in the middle of the night.

We struggled and often felt alone. I (Tony) was still trying to juggle my business and provide for the family, including all the new medical bills. At times, I felt like I might have a mental breakdown. I found myself being very angry all the time. I just had to put my head down and keep going. However, God always made sure someone was looking out for me, sometimes even strangers who would listen or say something encouraging that would get me through another day.

Looking back, we knew our friends and family were there, helping as much as they could. My (Kelly's) brothers come from a pastoral place and were always checking in on us and catching anything that they saw might be falling through the cracks.

We were also being shepherded beautifully by our church, with constant support from our pastors and our small group. They were very intentional and purposeful in asking us the right questions, even when we didn't want to answer them. It was not formal counseling, per se, but we definitely felt like people were paying attention. Although that didn't end our crisis, it no doubt helped us feel like we might one day be able to come out somewhat intact on the other end of this crisis.

CHAPTER 11

Ringing the Bell

(Tyler)

O steosarcoma is a freakishly fast-growing cancer. Doctors encountered a major issue within my first month of chemotherapy. From the time the original X-ray revealed my tumor to the time I started therapy, the tumor had grown from my humerus all the way up into my shoulder. They originally planned to do surgery on my humerus bone, but that plan had to change quickly. I now needed a shoulder replacement as well.

We just weren't able to outrun the pace of osteosarcoma.

I underwent something called a "reverse-shoulder surgery." A *reverse shoulder* is an implanted device that reverses the ball and the socket of the joint in your shoulder. At the time, there were only a few surgeons in the world who could do this procedure. Miraculously, one of them, Dr. Dan Wurtz, lived and practiced in Indianapolis.

He would travel all over the world to teach other people how to do the surgery because, essentially, it was a new approach that afforded patients the potential to regain a majority of their range of motion. This was especially significant for someone who was young and in need of a shoulder replacement.

The implanted appliance was made of titanium, a metal I would become very familiar with over time. Today, I have millions of dollars' worth of metal in my body from all the surgeries I've endured. This first surgery installed titanium from my shoulder all the way down to just above my elbow.

Needless to say, airports hate me. When TSA agents give me a hard time, I sometimes give them a hard time back, but I understand that if detecting hidden metal is your job, then I'm a just cause for hazard pay. One time, I faced a scary situation on my way back from a mission trip to China. The Chinese government detained me temporarily because they thought I was trying to sneak something illegal across the border. This is just one of the many unexpected surprises of being a bionic man.

I underwent chemo for four months before having the surgery, mainly to attempt to decrease the size and spread of the tumor. I woke up from my shoulder-replacement surgery to the welcome news that it had been successful—they had removed the entire tumor. I still had five months of chemo ahead of me, but I think that was the first break in the clouds I experienced—the first glimmer of hope that I might actually survive. In fact, just thinking of that moment makes me emotional to this day.

Four months may seem pretty short, but it is a long time to not know if you are going to live or die. But after the surgery, I had a renewed sense of peace. I felt that Christ was saying to me, "I've got you. You don't need to worry because I've got your back."

I began to crawl out of my depression as well, even before I had completely finished my treatments. I began to dream again. I dreamed of what life might look like down the road. Maybe I would get to go to college. Maybe I would be able to throw a ball again. Or a Frisbee.

Just maybe.

I reached out to the friends I had wounded and apologized for how I had treated them. Their willingness to understand and forgive taught me so much about the depth of divine love—a love that endures all things, including adolescent angst and chemotherapy.

After nine months of hell, I really did come out on the other side a new man. I was first diagnosed in July 2014, just before my sophomore year of high school. I entered remission in April 2015. It was shortly after this that I took the aforementioned trip to China to help kids there learn English. Yes, I had just been to hell and back, but I thankfully came back, so I was excited for an opportunity to share my story with people at home and overseas. I wanted them to experience the incredible grace I had just experienced firsthand.

April 17, 2015, was the day I was able to "ring the bell" at Riley Children's Hospital. I was in remission. The entire cancer ordeal seemed like a bad dream that I was ready to leave behind. I believed that I would never have to deal with this terrible disease again.

It was a great feeling, and I wanted it to last forever.

CHAPTER 12

Getting Back to the Future

(Tyler)

After I fully recovered from my shoulder surgery and the final rounds of my chemotherapy, I entered a season that is truly hard to describe. That's probably because so few people ever experience what I had been through.

By virtue of everything I had faced, as well as the fact that I was at the ripe old age of sixteen, I had already waved bye-bye to childhood forever. Regardless, I was able to regain a hint of childhood energy without the "childhood" being attached to it. In other words, I was able to dream again . . . to look forward into the great abyss of college, career, marriage, fatherhood, and the like, with a sense of hope. The black cloud of dread that had hovered above me for a year had finally dissipated. Some sunny skies were visible.

The Will to Hope

In terms of mental energy, attitude, and pursuits, it was time to pick myself up and get back to the future again.

Hope is a funny thing. Much research has been done regarding the power of a person's will to live, but I believe a huge part of the will to live comes from the will to hope. When hope exists, it doesn't mean that the future is guaranteed to be problem-free; it only means that you are able to see more options than just the one in front of you, or the one you most fear.

A person with hope might be in just as much of a place of uncertainty as anyone else, but he or she can envision and thus hope for other possibilities for the future. We can believe, even when we cannot yet see the object or outcome of the hope we are believing in.

I think most of us walk through life with a false sense of security because everything that could go wrong usually hasn't gone wrong—or at least it hasn't gone wrong yet. Most of us would never say the "yet" because we don't live expecting the worst, even though the only reason to believe that the worst is not a real possibility is the fact that it has not happened up to now. Even individuals who claim they are "worst-case scenario people" don't generally carry the weight of every possible worst-case scenario every minute of the day. How could they even take a breath, since the worst-case scenario is that they won't be able to?

In my case, a terrible scenario had actually happened to me, but I had lived through it. I could hope again, but I doubt that it was in the same way that many sixteen-year-olds hope for their futures. The known of my past was now an irremovable backdrop for the unknown of my future. It didn't eclipse my future—that is, I didn't want to just sit around waiting for the next bad thing to happen. But when you've already experienced the worst-case scenario, it's difficult to fully remove yourself from that trauma.

Long Days and Short Years

Sometime during remission, it felt as if God scooped up my past experiences, along with the perspectives and lessons I had learned through faith and the community around me, and used it all to lift me up and propel me toward a new philosophy of living. It became clearly evident to me that life should be about more than simply not dying. I didn't just want to live; I wanted to live *fully*.

Why do people not live their lives fully? It's a great question that a million books have addressed. One of those books would impact me greatly. It was called *When Breath Becomes Air* by Paul Kalanithi.

At the age of thirty-six and on the verge of completing a decade's worth of training as a neurosurgeon, Kalanithi was diagnosed with stage IV lung cancer. In one moment, Kalanithi went from being a doctor who examined the life and death of others to just another patient forced to face not just his own mortality, but also the meaning—or lack thereof—found in living. His examinations of life and death shifted from the mere physical or medical to something deeper. Something higher.

My examinations of what it meant not just to survive, but also to really live, changed as well. Even though I once again had hope for the future, I found myself more focused on the present. The present suddenly looked so much longer than the future.

Especially during adolescence, the future can often feel like a mass of events, emotions, accomplishments, and failures all tangled up in a ball that is positioned far enough away to be just beyond your ability to see it or grasp it. Mostly, you try to hope for it and not fear it—because you can't really see it.

I had not become a post-chemo psychic; that is, I could not suddenly see into the future. But I had become a person who could now see into the present.

Kalanithi observed from his own journey that "the days are long, but the years are short." No words could be truer for me. The days during chemotherapy in which I felt like I had no future were excruciatingly long and painful, both physically and mentally. But now, I could actually see that long days were also the greatest gifts I had to work with. Days were vehicles that brought the opportunities to live a life full of possibilities.

Returning to the Present

Some of this newfound appreciation for the present meant returning to normalcy in a few areas. I was able to reengage my studies in the way I had before being sick. Academics were never difficult for me—it all came to me naturally. So I was able to return to my natural nerdy habitat of reading, writing, and studying.

I was also able to return to hanging out with my friends from school and church, engaging in anything and everything we could do that might be fun. This included epic battles of wit and fortitude— also known as board games. I'm kind of a legend when it comes to winning board games. It has been suggested that I might be just a little bit competitive—and whoever said this might be more than just a little bit right. Regardless, being able to again engage in these silly, seemingly unimportant things was huge for me.

I also regained the joy of conversation with my friends and family. People always said that I smiled a lot as a kid, and I liked that. Smiling is a way to show what I am feeling or choosing a way to transfer these feelings to other people, too. During my cancer treatments, I had smiled a lot less. I set out to make up for lost time. Yes, I did have a great reason to smile again, but it was not just because I had entered into remission.

It would be easy to sum things up and say that my bout with cancer had changed me, but I think this would be too simple a summation. The truth is, it was God who changed me through the process of living through cancer. Again, cancer deserves no credit and will not get any from me. My outlook on life after my battle with cancer changed so drastically that I really don't think a simple "coming of age as you face your mortality" description suffices.

I was not just coming of age . . . it was during this time that I was truly coming to faith. My relationship with Christ began changing from adolescent study and theory into a real relationship, complete with real conversations, real disappointments, real disagreements, and real trust.

Good vs. Bad

I'm no philosopher, but I have been to where most people would consider the very cliffs overlooking one of life's greatest injustices—childhood cancer. It was there that I discovered where my own human expectation of good actually comes from.

If I'm being honest, I think somewhere deep down inside, I had emotionally interpreted my diagnosis in the early days as some sort of punishment from God for all the mistakes I had made. If you're being honest, I'll bet this might not be too unfamiliar of a concept to you, either. I couldn't have been more wrong, but it sure felt like a valid explanation in the moment. My experience caused me to take a closer examination of the way I looked at what is good and what is bad because if I had the feeling that I was being punished for not being good enough, then what exactly did I think "good" meant in the first place?

The definition of *good* certainly varies from person to person, but we all have a definition. You might not think it is wrong to do a certain thing that someone else thinks is wrong, but I guarantee that there is something someone else could do to you that you would think is wrong, whether stealing your possessions, hurting your family, or doing something else harmful to you. We all think something is wrong, even if we don't share the reasoning for it. It is this kind of concept of right and wrong—and of good and bad—that strongly suggests we have something going on inside of us beyond just an instinctive, evolutionary desire to survive and advance.

If everything is just random and there is no real reason for us to have a concept of good, bad, right, or wrong, then why do we become so surprised and upset when a child or a "good person" gets cancer? Why does this kind of suffering feel different to us than other kinds? What is it that makes us shake our heads and ask, "Why do bad things happen to good people?" The animals out in the wild don't seem to be asking this question, but we certainly are.

Why does a certain thing feel like such an injustice unless somewhere within us, we have an expectation of justice, something not found elsewhere in nature? And if it's not found in nature, where does it come from?

Discovering Grace

Again, I had been to a horrible cliff where injustice seemed to abound; but surprisingly, it was there that my *childish* faith was thrown over the ledge, and I was given an invaluable replacement— a *childlike* faith. I don't have to worry about you thinking that I'm proclaiming my own goodness or perfection here because now you know that I do not consider myself more worthy than anyone else. No, I have discovered something even better than an explanation for why "bad things happen to good people" . . . something better than right or wrong.

I discovered grace.

Grace changed me, not cancer. Grace never turned its back on me, even when I didn't deserve it. Instead, God poured out his patient love on me in greater amounts, even as I doubted him and wondered if he remembered or cared about me.

Grace taught me where my entitled human expectation for good things actually comes from—I inherited it as a result of sharing the image of the one who, in the very beginning, made all things good. We were created for good, which is why we instinctively expect good and also why "bad" feels so foreign and disappointing every single time. This is why we cry out for justice, even if our standards for doing so vary—it is because we know we are supposed to be good, but something is wrong.

Cancer proves that something is indeed wrong. Things are not as they should be. But grace teaches us that God did not originally intend these wrongs for us. He begs us not to poison our own world with such things—and we do it anyway. Despite this, he still cares about the ways we suffer under our own wrongs, so much so that God came down where we are to experience the crushing weight of our wrongs, a weight he didn't deserve. Out of his vast love for us, he died to pay for our wrongs—and then he conquered death itself, the thing we fear the most, when he came back to life.

Grace teaches us that God has written us into his eternal story of making all these wrongs right again.

The real issue is time. We are not yet to the next chapter of the eternal story, so we can't understand why so many bad things keep happening. We can't see that the chapter we live in is quite short in light of an endless story. "For this light momentary affliction is preparing for us an eternal weight of glory beyond all comparison . . ." (2 Corinthians 4:17, ESV).

Light? Momentary? I've suffered from a painful cancer that seems anything but light and momentary. I don't think God is making "light" of our difficulties—there's another way to see it. If what is to come is so superior to what we know today that, by comparison, even the worst things we can experience now are considered light and momentary compared to then, can you even imagine how incredible this future must be?

But we lose sight of this in the middle of our pain. I get it. We even say things like, "If God is so good, then why does he allow all these bad things to happen to innocent people?" We miss the fact that we are the culprits and that Christ was the resulting victim of our crimes, not the other way around. He is innocent, not us.

When I realized that youth didn't entitle me to anything, much less life and health, I began to realize the incredible gift of grace that every moment of my life truly was. Yes, I want a healthy life for myself and for every child and family in the world. I want to eradicate this terrible disease. I work toward this goal with all my might. However, I no longer believe that I don't deserve cancer; rather, I realize that I have never deserved any of the life I have been graced with in the first place. I have been graced with grace.

There certainly is a great deal of mystery to God's sovereignty and to what he allows to happen, as well as to the time he keeps allowing to pass before finally turning the page to the next chapter and finishing his ultimate work of setting all this wrong back to right. The mystery is great, but I now know that it is not mine to solve. This means I have finally accepted that I am limited and finite and that this is not an injustice—because I am loved, despite my own injustice.

I am completely known, yet I am completely loved.

So life and death no longer revolve around just living or dying. If this world is temporary, then I no longer want to relate to it in my heart in permanent ways. I can enjoy it, but I don't want to galvanize it as my only hope. I will work hard, but I will do so with a sense of rest. This was the transformation through the grace of Christ that I began to walk in during my time of remission.

Into the Great Unknown

My personality is such that I really enjoy going out and doing things that are outside my norm. I guess you could say I'm an *experience* person, not a *picture* person. I would rather live *in* the moment so that I can really experience it than stop to pose for a picture of it.

Now that you understand what God was doing in my life during this time, it will be no surprise to learn that my junior and senior years of high school were filled with adventure.

My family took a Make-A-Wish trip to Hawaii, which was amazing. I hung out with my friends—a lot. We laughed until we cried. We played board games until we were blue in the face. We stayed up late, took day trips, and went on hikes—and I always tried to push the envelope by staying at the front of the group, setting the pace and the tone as I lived it up with the ones I loved, the ones who would most appreciate where I now was, in light of where I once had been.

I felt like a dead man who lived to tell about it. I wanted to move. I wanted to breathe. I wanted to live. The whole season was amazing . . . and I "raced slowly" through it, living each day as fully as possible, twisting and wringing out the potential that saturated every moment, drinking life to the dregs.

Again, the days were long, but the years were short.

Before I knew it, graduation was approaching. It was time to begin taking steps into the future I had once possessed, lost, and had now found again.

I am thankful that school has always been easy for me. I was even humbled to learn that I scored very high on my SAT, which would help open doors for the next season of my education. As an academically inclined person, the idea of college was a joyful non-negotiable of my future.

I don't think college is for everyone, especially considering the amount of debt you can quickly accumulate. But for me, the act of going away to college was a beacon of light in my future that had been beckoning me toward it ever since middle school. I would say it was like a moth to a flame, but more accurately, it's like a bookworm to a library. It's not as catchy, but you get the idea.

I deeply desired to walk across a campus carrying a backpack full of textbooks that I might or might not have read—because I would finally have the chance to try "winging it" in a class, if I wanted to. I wanted to stay up late being goofy with my friends, only to stumble into an 8:00 a.m. class the next morning. I wanted to live in a disgustingly messy dorm with wild roommates and experience freshman-floor shenanigans. I wanted to exhaust all the points on my prepaid meal plan. I wanted to then eat cheap ramen like so many other college vagrants. I wanted to learn. I wanted to grow. I wanted to stretch my legs and spread my wings.

You see, the very idea of the college experience itself was a huge deal for me. I felt like my high school experience had been marked by cancer, and I hoped that my college experience might be more "normal," whatever that might mean.

This season of my life was characterized by college decisions—and as is probably the case for most nearly graduated seniors, it became quite the saga. I know that now I have gained a reputation as a Purdue "super-fan," but growing up, I was *not* a Purdue fan. (Insert here the deafening sounds of crickets.)

Many Purdue fans have asked me what childhood trauma or nefariously altered state of consciousness could ever force a young boy living an hour from West Lafayette to cheer for IU—especially one who was living under the secure roof of a loving father who was a Purdue alumnus. I have no tragic story to share. My reason was much less dramatic, and perhaps also a little mischievous. You see, I just really like to push people's buttons. My dark confession is that I think I cheered for Indiana simply to give Dad a hard time.

Scratch that. I *know* that's why I did it.

Call it loving banter. Call it inner-family rivalry. Call it whatever you want, but I really enjoyed busting my dad's chops, and the best way I found to do that was to put on crimson and cream and cheer for the Hoosiers. Sure, it drove him crazy—ironically, I think it made him want to throw a chair farther than Bobby Knight.

But now that it was almost time to go to college, all choices seemed pretty valid. To cover all my bases, I applied to three different schools: Purdue, Indiana, and North Carolina State. When you're a statistician, you're a super-fan of backup plans—it's almost as if you constantly hear in the back of your mind the voice of Effie Trinket from *The Hunger Games* encouraging you in a tone that sounds like a warning: "May the odds be ever in your favor."

After all I had been through up to that point, when there was even a possibility that I could affect the odds, I did my best to do so.

I was accepted at all three schools, which was an honor and a relief. My college visits began with Indiana. There was no real specific reason, but it became apparent to me after a little time on IU's campus that it wasn't where I needed to be. I mean no offense to Indiana alumni and fans; it just didn't feel right for me.

The most determining factor in my college decision, however, was not a campus but the fact that I wanted to pursue the study of data analytics. One of the best programs in the nation for this field is at North Carolina State University. After a visit there, my heart became fully fixated on NC State.

Besides their stellar data analytics program, it is such a beautiful campus, surrounded by beautiful landscapes. It's close to mountains and great beaches—what's not to love? We also have long-term family friends who are associated with the university, so there are some familiar people there.

Furthermore, it is the school where the legendary Jimmy Valvano once coached the men's basketball team to an unlikely national championship. He lost his physical battle with cancer, but his story remains one of the greatest upset narratives in modern history. The area boasts one of the largest cancer research centers in America, and since I was already serious about using my story, my voice, and my life to truly affect the collective fight against cancer, it seemed to be a perfect fit. It was about ten hours away from home, which would be a pretty big change for me and my family, but I was undeterred.

I was ready to launch out into the deep. And things became even better when I learned that I was in the final running to receive a full ride to NC State. Everything was shaping up nicely . . . until it wasn't.

I was not picked for the full-ride scholarship, which was a huge disappointment. Even so, I figured that since I had been in the running for the university's largest scholarship, surely I would now be a leading candidate for other sizable scholarships. Sure enough, they offered me a significant scholarship, and it appeared that NC State was going to work out because I could now afford to go there without being a financial burden to my parents or to my future self. They offered me the scholarship on a Friday, and I emailed them my acceptance on Sunday.

Then Monday rolled around.

I received an email stating that there had been a mix-up. I was actually *not* qualified for the scholarship they had offered me because our family was not in enough financial need. I am so grateful that needs-based scholarships exist as a much-needed resource for those who can't afford to attend college, but for myself in that moment, the news was a hard pill to swallow. I had my heart set on NC State. I know it was an honest mistake, but in the moment, I was sorely disappointed.

On Thursday, NC State sent another email offering me a scholarship of much lesser value. The same day, my grandfather—my mom's stepdad—was diagnosed with cancer. We were devastated.

When Obstacles Become Guardrails

The whole admission process had become a season of difficulty and confusion—layered with another cancer diagnosis within my family. But I would soon learn that it was also a season of divine protection and direction in ways I simply could not see at the moment.

Isn't that often how it works? You feel like you're wandering through a dark place, looking for a way out. As you search for an exit, you keep painfully running into some unidentifiable object that is hard with rough, sharp edges. Running into it hurts, so you begin to resent this unknown obstacle, eventually even hating it and blaming it for your situation.

You become frustrated that God would allow this obstacle to continually block your progress and also cause you so much pain. But one day, the lights get turned on, and you discover that the obstacle you despised and resented so much in the dark is actually a guardrail in the light. And just beyond the guardrail is a cliff from which you would have stumbled into danger and pain far greater than the guardrail you hated so much.

The scholarship offer to NC State simply wasn't enough money for me to afford attending there. My parents raised me to work hard and, as much as possible, avoid debt. So I knew that from the outset of my adulthood, I needed to be wise with my money. I didn't want to strap my future wife and kids with what would amount to hundreds of thousands of dollars of college debt. It was a hole that would be difficult to dig out of, no matter how much money I might end up making after college.

Becoming a Boilermaker

On Friday, one day later, I committed to Purdue—the familiar school only an hour away from home; they extended to me the generous offer of the Presidential scholarship. Living so close to Purdue, I had visited the campus many times with my dad over the years. I knew what it was all about.

I was now a Boilermaker, and there was no looking back. You can imagine all the ways my dad and I volleyed our playful banter back and forth. The prodigal son was returning home and away from the pigpen of IU. (Forgive me, IU readers—you are being thrown into our playful banter.)

Dad was hilariously relentless in giving me a hard time about it, but after a lifetime of dishing it, taking it was well deserved. The truth is, I knew it meant a lot to him because deep down inside, I think he always hoped that at least one of his kids would go to Purdue. After all we had been through, I know it made him proud that his oldest son would be a Boilermaker, just like him.

As soon as I had finally committed and the college search saga was over, things felt right. Even though Purdue didn't have the program of study I was looking for, something inside me knew this was God's direction.

A couple of weeks later, Purdue announced the creation and launch of a new data analytics program of their own. I was ecstatic! This added yet another layer to what God has been teaching me at every turn in my unpredictable story—that despite the best efforts of a spiritual enemy and my frustration and questioning, God knows what he is doing and will redeem everything—even the bad things—for my ultimate good.

After driving a hundred circular laps on the roundabout of decision, I ended up turning again onto my own street, so to speak. I was staying close to home. It was actually a good feeling, even though I had thought I would be going to school out of state. My heart felt right about being at Purdue. I was poised to enter college with a renewed sense of confidence in God's grace extended to me.

CHAPTER 13

A Different Kind of Chaos

(Tony & Kelly)

Tyler's remission was different from what we expected. We imagined that life would return to normal, and in some ways it did. But it's hard to know what normal is when you are already in the middle of all the regular changes happening in the lives of three teenage boys.

There was always a hidden fear lodged somewhere deep down in our souls. It would raise its head when we would go in for his checkups every three months. It was like that feeling you get when you keep looking back over your shoulder to see if something is following you. The feeling lessened each time we heard he was still cancer-free, but it was always there.

Life turned into a flurry of crazy activity *not* related to cancer. Tyler had been out of the hospital for only about a month before he headed to China on a mission trip. This was such a big deal for him because it meant he was returning to being a part of the adventures his friends were experiencing.

But for me (Kelly), the summer of 2015 was horrible. I sank into a deep, dark depression that I am pretty sure was caused by post-traumatic stress. My mind, body, and spirit were all simply spent. I felt run down. I struggled to have the emotional energy to reestablish even the simplest of routines at home. I had given everything I had to my family during our year of cancer. I was spent.

At this point, our kids were changing rapidly, so we all had to reconnect in the new context and find our bearings for this season of life. This included our Make-A-Wish adventure trip to Hawaii, but quite honestly, I don't remember much about it. Our year of cancer had taken us out of so many of our normal activities at church and other places, so we struggled to get involved again. I know it sounds weird, but I really can't recall what life was like during that period.

I think I no longer knew who I was.

I had tried to homeschool all the kids during the whole cancer ordeal, but that happened only in theory because I was always tending to Tyler. We had a lot of friends step up to help us with school. Ethan was in the fourth grade and Blake was in the eighth grade. Blake was struggling academically. This was new to me from a homeschooling perspective because by sixth grade, Tyler was almost completely independent academically. Blake was gifted, but he was wired very differently than Tyler. Homeschooling during that time was utter chaos to the point that eventually we sent both Ethan and Blake to public school instead. It just worked better for each of their unique lives and personalities.

I didn't set out to homeschool at all—it just kind of happened. I graduated from Ball State University as a psychology major before working as an admissions counselor and then at an in-house rehab facility for a couple of years. That really wasn't what I wanted to do, so I worked as a nanny for four years before we began having our own kids. I loved being a caretaker, especially for children. The timing was perfect—I was transitioning out of my nanny job just as I was about to give birth to Tyler.

Again, it was never in my original plans to homeschool, but I agreed to do it in the beginning because Tony felt pretty strongly about it. Our original plan was that we would do it only for Tyler's kindergarten year, just to see how it would go. Well, that did not go exactly according to plan; Tyler ended up graduating high school as a homeschooler.

Homeschooling worked for me because taking care of people—

especially my family—is just the way I am wired. I was made to be a caregiver, so Tyler's situation took me to the very brink; I gave everything I had to take care of him and our family. I felt the pain and uncertainty of the situation in such a deep way that it left a crater inside of me. It was as if I had been to war and just couldn't adjust to life during peacetime.

I (Tony) regret the way I felt during this time because I actually harbored bitterness toward Kelly when she entered into her depression. I understood why she was struggling, but when she seemed to shut down, I became completely overwhelmed with keeping everything in our lives from falling apart. Between all the family chaos of having three sons, the ongoing emotional recovery process at home, and keeping up with my business, a season that should have felt so relieving was filled with many unexpected, difficult moments.

We want to share these experiences hopefully to inspire you to be there for others in the right way, even after the initial trauma has occurred. We were out of the woods in one capacity, but there was still so much adjustment we struggled to make, so much of an equilibrium we struggled to regain. You might be that someone who pays attention enough to keep reaching out when others assume all is well—those "someones" made a difference at many points in our journey.

The chaos of Tyler's cancer had passed, but a general sense of chaos itself never seemed to leave us.

CHAPTER 14

Shooting (Pain) from the Hip

(Tyler)

W hen I entered the final semester of my senior year of high school, the future felt incredibly bright. I knew where I was going to college. I knew what I wanted to study. I even had an idea of what I wanted to be: a statistician and sports writer.

I knew all these things, but I had to deal yet again with an old traveling partner—the fear of the unknown. It is an unwelcome stowaway, but none of us can fully throw it overboard for good. You might rid yourself of it for a day or even for a longer period of time, but it always worms its way back on board.

Living in remission was obviously an incredibly refreshing, exciting, and hopeful season. But there was another side to being a cancer survivor that carried with it something heavier. It was a weight I tried to carry in my back pocket so that I wouldn't always feel it or hopefully even notice it, but it was always still there.

It was a constant, achy sense of dread about the possibility that my cancer might someday return.

I don't believe that the sheer act of considering the possibility revealed a lack of faith in what God had done for me. That same logic in reverse would lead one to the conclusion that a lack of faith caused the cancer in the first place. This really wasn't about a lack or a presence of faith in a good outcome. My faith was now in Christ, regardless of the outcome. But the bottom line was that such a possibility was simply a reality of living in a broken world. It was a reality I prayed would never materialize, but it was still never far from my mind.

Speed Bumps and Whispers

Fear is a whisperer, and it has *a lot* to say. Like all whispering, it is easier to hear when everything else is still and quiet. It's a good thing that my disposition since childhood has led me to rarely slow down and be quiet. Staying on the move is not only just a reflection of my temperament; it also helps me keep the ambient volume of a full life cranked up louder than the whispering fear of the unknown. Yes, I still hear it—and I definitely heard it a lot during this season of remission—but I tried not to listen.

It whispered the same old things: *Could this cancer nightmare happen again? If it keeps coming back, will it finally kill me?*

Over time, I had gained some incredible friends in the cancer community who walked similar paths. They became my comrades. They are a huge reason I am writing this book in the first place—not just to shine light on my own story, but also on theirs. They are my heroes.

I have lost friends to cancer, including one of my really good friends, Angelo Wilford, who died on December 10, 2016. He finally succumbed to death because his body simply could not tolerate the chemotherapy any longer. All told, he went into remission and relapsed three times. Outside of his family, I was one of the last people to visit him before his death.

Being present at someone's deathbed is an experience that stays with you.

We're all driving on the road of life, and there are *a lot* of speed bumps along the way—difficulties and frustrations in our lives. If you hit one of these speed bumps while driving fast, everything in your car, including your body, gets thrown about and jostled. Everything not sealed or secured will spill.

The flip side is that if you go over a speed bump while driving slowly, it won't necessarily be a smooth ride, but it should be much less tumultuous. To me, going slowly means, as much as possible, living life one day at a time.

I am a planner, so I like to prepare for things as far in advance as possible. My eyes are almost always looking far down the road. So this realization that I should slow down and approach life one day at a time has not been easy for me. I would rather floor it. But through these experiences, I have tried to learn to slow my ride and not worry as much about the speed bumps I might encounter a year down the road. Instead, I try to focus on those that are right before me today.

Oh, and I try to make sure that everything in my "car" is secured. Fast or slow, speed bumps are coming for every single one of us. I want to have my confidence and motivations constantly secured, not by wishful thinking, blind faith, or oblivious living, but by something that can hold me in place when everything around me goes flying.

I'm not sure about my speed of life at the time, but I was about to hit a major speed bump . . . and the contents of our lives were about to go flying. Again.

No Day at the Beach

In January 2017, during my senior year, I took a little vacation with my parents to Florida. When you are homeschooled and your dad owns Trent Companies, Inc. (a professional landscaping company), January is a great month to get away from it all, which includes the harsh Indiana winters.

We traveled and met up with our friends, the Osbourne family. Their son, Noah, has been one of my best friends for most of my life. His sister, Anni, is also one of my closest friends; she is also like a sister to me. The three of us spent a lot of time that trip on the beach engaged in a game called Spikeball.

During one of these games, Noah had a really great shot that necessitated me running fast after the ball. When I did, I pulled or strained something in my groin. At the time, it seemed to be nothing but a common, minor sports injury.

But for the rest of the trip and then for weeks afterward, my groin pain persisted and worsened. We finally went to see a chiropractor about it. After his multiple treatments still didn't help me improve, we finally went to the hospital for an X-ray, just to make sure nothing else was going on.

The old familiar whisper suddenly became a lot louder during the hospital visit. But the X-ray revealed that all was well. Nothing alarming was found on the scan, so the doctors felt that it truly was just some sort of muscle strain. I was so relieved. Now I could get back to my senior year and stop worrying about this persistent injury.

But after a couple more weeks had passed, the pain still had not. In fact, it had become progressively worse. I was now walking with a noticeable limp, to the point that people were constantly asking me about it.

So we went back to the hospital yet again; at this point, it was late March. They ordered an MRI in order to pinpoint the exact nature of my injury so that they could treat it directly.

The whisper came back again, but there was no ignoring it this time because in a matter of a few hours, it would morph into a terrifying scream.

The MRI revealed that a tumor was growing on my pelvis. Unfortunately, when we had gone in for the first X-ray several weeks before, the scan had shown only the outside of my hip. This tumor was on the inside. My pelvis hid it from the initial scan. The tumor was pushing against my leg and the surrounding joints, which was causing all the pain I was feeling when I walked.

It was cancer. Again.

CHAPTER 15

The New Hardest Thing

(Tony)

I always thought the hardest thing I would ever have to do was tell my child that he had cancer. I was wrong . . . telling him he had cancer *again* was much worse.

The look on my boy's face was one of shock and devastation. It wrecked me in a way I didn't realize was possible. I can still see the look on his face—the realization that he had to face this all over again. It is something I'll have to live with for the rest of my life, almost as if I had seen something on a battlefield that can never be unseen. I was angry—which included being angry at God—that we had to go through this again.

I am not proud of everywhere my mind went. There were moments when I wanted to just walk out the door and never come back—to leave my family behind and move to Colorado or somewhere else far away so that I could stop feeling this unbearable pain over and over again. I would get on my scooter and go out for long rides, hoping a car would hit me head-on and get me out of this situation. I was desperate, and there is no sense in hiding the depth of despair I felt.

It was tragically true once again—we *all* got cancer for a second time.

CHAPTER 16

The Pain of New Opportunities

(Tyler)

C*ancer.*
It felt like I had just awakened from a bad dream only to find I was actually in a bigger bad dream. I couldn't see the look on my face, but I could see by the sheer devastation reflected in my parents' eyes that theirs had to be worse than mine. The initial shock wave of the news was devastating. It was a terrible feeling that I knew wouldn't just subside, but rather would continue to create tidal wave upon tidal wave of emotion.

Anger. Fear. Disbelief. You name it; we felt it.

A Heart Set on August

People have often asked about my first thought when I found out that my cancer had returned. Truthfully, my first thought was simple: *No matter what, I have to go to Purdue in the fall.*

Being able to be on campus when classes were slated to begin was my highest concern. I know this might sound trite in light of the fact that I was again facing life and death, but again, I didn't just want to survive . . . I wanted to really live, to thrive. And at that moment in time, going to college was the most important practical goal of living beyond survival.

School became my primary focus of prayer every day. I would pray, "Lord, whatever you need to do between now and the fall, please do it. Whatever it takes, you already know it and that I'm open to doing it. So please just allow me to start school in the fall." I knew that God was working out the right timing for everything, but my desire for God to answer this timing request was so intense that I couldn't imagine him not answering it.

It may have been June in Carmel, but my heart was already living in August in West Lafayette.

Cancer was obviously *the* setback, but missing school would have felt like my life itself was being pushed back into some sort of childhood state I could never escape. Even if my health situation was abnormal, I just wanted to keep living as normally as possible. The other thing was that I had fully committed to Purdue. If I say yes to something, I'm going to do it. Period.

During my first bout with cancer, I had almost lost and regained almost everything that mattered to me, including my life. But there was one thing I never wanted to regain from that first experience: my excuses. I had decided I was going to be someone who followed through on every "yes." I would keep my word at all costs, just as Christ told us all: "[L]et your 'Yes' be 'Yes,' and your 'No,' 'No'" (Matthew 5:37, NKJV).

This wasn't just a principled stance for me. There were also actual people I would fail if I didn't make it to college in the fall, like a friend named John Kruse. He was a cool guy I met on Facebook. We were both looking for a roommate at the time, so we met up for dinner and a Cubs game in Chicago to discuss it. We hit it off and that was that— and I was still dedicated to keeping *that* exactly as we had agreed. I owed it to him. People had taken care of me so many times, so I had to do my part to take care of others too, regardless of my condition.

I had also been looking forward to college for a long time, including all the experiences that would come along with it. Despite the news I had just received, I focused on this goal because school gave me something very tangible to shoot for as we once again began evaluating my treatment options.

The second diagnosis hit us on a Friday. Obviously, my doctors wanted to make up for lost time and move as quickly as possible. So the next Wednesday, I was back in the hospital for a biopsy. By Friday of the same week, the diagnosis of osteosarcoma was confirmed. Then the next Monday, I was in the hospital receiving my first round of chemotherapy. We were off to the races yet again, attempting to outrun the speedy cancer inside me.

Typically, with my first experience of chemotherapy, I would receive one round over a time period of three to five days. The amount of time people usually spend in the hospital during these kinds of treatments usually depends on the type and severity of their cancer. My general experience during my first bout with cancer was to stay three or four days for a single dose of chemotherapy and then be released to go home.

But this time around, I had to stay in the hospital for five days straight, and on every single one of those days, I received a single dose of chemotherapy. Their preliminary method of fighting my relapse was to load me up with a lot of chemo on the front end—ten rounds—with the hope that it would work its painful "magic" over a longer period of time.

And because I was a relapse patient, I went through an entire chemotherapy regimen not just once, but twice.

Osteosarcoma and chondrosarcoma are the two most common forms of bone cancer, but they are actually pretty rare in occurrence compared to other non-bone cancers. This unfortunately means that there has been less testing, and thus less useful research and data, focused on these specific cancers.

This makes things more difficult because treatment options are very limited—*especially* if it's a relapse. Because I relapsed, all the doctors at Riley viewed my first regimented plan and course of chemotherapy to be a failure. In other words, they felt that they couldn't give me the same drugs again because they didn't work the first time. As I learned more about what I was up against this time around, something else was birthed within me: a relentless desire to find a cure for osteosarcoma.

There is only one certified treatment in the United States for osteosarcoma, which generally involves possible amputation, followed by chemotherapy. During my first bout, even though my arm did not require amputation, this was still the treatment path I endured. And by their standards, it had failed. So for my new tumor, this meant we had a couple of different options, including the use of clinical trials. Such a course would help with insurance because clinical trials are usually covered. When it was all said and done, our doctors actually strongly recommended following Europe's first line of treatment, which included a different set of chemotherapy drugs than the ones we used the first time around.

It helped that Riley Children's Hospital was one of the few hospitals in the nation actively participating in precision genomics with its patients. If one of Riley's patients was recommended for the program and then also selected after a series of evaluations, a biological sample of his or her tumor would be sent off to a facility in Arizona, where scientists would test and study its DNA and the RNA. Their purpose was to attempt to identify a highly specific treatment plan that would be tailored according to the specific data of each person's tumor.

Every person's cancer is a unique puzzle, like an encoded message. This means each person's cancer can be best treated—or decoded—through the use of a key or cipher specific to the individual's own internal puzzle. The resulting treatment is to use a specific drug or sequence of drugs to treat a person's specific tumor. It is a targeted approach rather than a generic one because when it comes to cancer, one size does not fit all.

Traditional chemotherapy typically targets all the rapidly developing cells in the body. This is why people lose their hair, and at times, their fingernails and toenails as well—the chemo attacks and kills both good cells and bad cells together. Conversely, precision genomics attempts to treat just the tumor itself.

This is such an important area of oncology that needs a drastic increase in research and funding. Cancer treatment is not cheap. Before you even make it to the treatment stage, you can already find yourself buried under a financial avalanche. Just the DNA test itself on my tumor cost $30,000—and we were just getting started on the second leg of my cancer journey.

For these expenses specifically, we were overwhelmed when, by God's provision, all of it was covered because Riley chose to enroll me in the precision genomics study. Specifically, Riley, the P.S. We Love You Fund, and the research center in Arizona where the testing occurred graciously covered all of these expenses.

My gratitude to them is eternal.

Each cycle within the genomic therapy plan was twenty-one days long. I would go in on the first day for a two-hour infusion before being allowed to go home. At home, I would take oral chemotherapy every evening—four pills before bed. On the eighth day, I would get another infusion before finishing out the twenty-one-day cycle on just the oral chemotherapy. Eventually, the whole sequence would start all over again. Thankfully, this therapy didn't seem to affect me as badly as traditional chemo in terms of negative side effects.

Same Problem . . . Different Me

After the initial shock of the diagnosis wore off a bit, I found a strange, unexpected sense of clarity. God had proven himself to me many times, even making sure that I enrolled at Purdue, where, little did I know at the time, I would be able to undergo my chemotherapy while also pursuing my education. While I was scared about the possible outcomes and uncertainties of this journey, my confidence in the Lord had deepened.

Don't get me wrong—I definitely felt and dealt with a lot of raw emotion during this season. I had just made a college decision; my grandfather—my mom's stepdad—had just been diagnosed with cancer; and now we were dealing with my second cancer diagnosis. The one happy thing bookended by two very sad things created space for a lot of difficult emotional moments in me and in my family. But even so, and it's hard to explain, my confidence had definitely changed.

I had some experience with this cancer process, so I'm sure that helped. I knew what it felt like to go through chemotherapy, and while I was not looking forward to it again, I had less fear of its unknowns. I was also older now, looking at the experience with adult eyes.

Above all, the closeness in my relationship with Christ was so different. Yes, I experienced anger and confusion, but instead of isolating myself and treating the whole situation as if God was abandoning me out of ambivalence or anger, I brought my anger, fear, and confusion *to* him.

I learned that I didn't have to understand to trust. Consider the complete trust and honest expression of a newborn. She may know nothing about her situation, and she's so willing to scream and cry out with her fussiness, anger, hunger, or fear—but somehow, those expressions to her father and mother bring them all closer to each other.

I had learned that I could be authentic, not just with other people, but also with Christ. I could question him without denying him. I could speak directly, even harshly, to him without abandoning my faith in him. I didn't have to fake a religious self—I could be my actual self. Faith is not the absence of real, visceral emotions and expressions toward God. Instead, it is the bringing of these emotions and expressions to God out of both an existing, imperfect trust and a desire to grow deeper in this trust.

We often talk about the ways that God uses difficulty to make us stronger, but we often miss one of the purposes for gaining more strength: to use it in the next difficult situation. In the military, greater strength better equips soldiers to handle tougher situations and enemies. In football, greater strength means better chances that a player will be put onto the field when the team's back is against the wall and the game is on the line.

I believe that we shouldn't believe any differently when we survive something difficult and come out stronger on the other side. While we don't go looking for more trouble, if and when it does come, we will find that the strength we gained back then wasn't forged in us for just *that* moment of difficulty, but also for the *next* moment of difficulty.

What a difference two years makes.

I think one of the biggest gifts of my life up to now is the passage of time and occurrence of events that convinced me that I can—and should—mentally separate God's personal nature, whether he is good or bad, from the single variable of my own life's situation, whether it is good or bad. I think this is how most people live. If we are experiencing what seem to be good circumstances, then God seems to be good. But when we are experiencing what seem to be bad circumstances, then the very nature of God suddenly comes into question in a way it wasn't before. God seems to be bad.

Above all else, we make definitive conclusions about the essence of the universe we can't even fully see, much less understand, based on the variables of what is happening to us personally on Earth, right now.

When we live this way, we evaluate God not by the eternally fixed attributes declared about him in creation, history, and scripture, but rather by the most constantly changing thing there is: our own feelings. Even if you don't fully trust scripture, you can probably at least agree that your feelings have proven to be untrustworthy as well. I'm not saying that our feelings are not valid; I'm just saying that somewhere along the way, I began to trust in a God who was much, much bigger than whatever may happen to me on this earth during the brief time I pass through this temporary life.

Billions of others have been right where I am, having been born, suffered, and eventually died, but it is all too easy to dismiss all their wisdom and insight in favor of my own personal limited experience right now. Whether my life is 25 or 105 years long, my perspective is still less than microscopic in the scope of all time, space, and eternity.

So why should I live as if I can fully and accurately make *the* definitive judgment about the mysteries of God in my own little lifetime and according to my own little life's ups and downs, even if my "downs" seemingly drop lower than someone else's? Why would I think a question so profound that has been studied, researched, and even debated from the likes of Aristotle, Augustine, and Aquinas to the likes of Luther, Locke, and Lucado, is suddenly solely mine to fully solve in less than twenty years of my life in the twenty-first century?

I guess I found out that I can't just Google my way to complete enlightenment.

My first battle against cancer helped me to see that everyone has a battle, so I shouldn't make my own the center of the universe. Even if it feels like it is because it consumes all my time, energy, and hopes for the future, it is not. Thinking or feeling something does not make it so. I should use my own battle to help others in theirs.

The reality is, everyone has a story. Everyone. And while the details and difficulties vary greatly from person to person, the fact remains that none of our individual stories define the realities of the universe. We can take to social media or simply to conversations to declare ourselves the center of the story. But we still ironically make these declarations not from the center we claim, but from the edges of the bigger story. Our stories might be important, but they are not the center.

I think it was during this season that I really began to understand what Paul meant when he said, "For me to live is Christ, and to die is gain" (Philippians 1:21, ESV). So for me, either way, I win. I'm either in heaven with Jesus or here on Earth with those I love.

I know it might sound strange, but I began to think of my second cancer diagnosis as a second chance. No, it was not a chance that I would have wanted, but since it was here anyway, I found a certain joy in knowing that I could do things differently this time around.

Everything is an opportunity—even cancer. I felt that I had wasted my first opportunity with cancer. In fact, when I was talking with someone about my relapse, I found myself saying something that was quite strange: I said that I was excited to have another opportunity to do things right. I was not excited about cancer, but I was excited about the chance to be the person of faith and grace that God had been developing.

Above all, I set out to approach relationships differently this time. I was worried about the side effects of the chemotherapy, which I know greatly contributed to this issue back in 2015. One of my early hospital stays during the second round caused me to have flashbacks to those relationship issues. Yes, I had reconciled with most of those people back then by talking to them. But to ensure that I handled things differently this time, I decided to write letters of apology to them again. I mailed them from the hospital.

It might have been the precision genomic therapy or just my ability to know what to expect, but it seemed that I was able to tolerate the side effects of chemotherapy better this time. It was still extremely difficult, but I learned to communicate better *before* I tanked into an emotional place. I still made my share of mistakes here, but I grew significantly in being able to better recognize when I was not feeling well so that I could warn my family instead of blowing up at them.

I would try to slow down and say, "Just so you know, I'm very irritable, so I'm going to go upstairs to hang out in my room for a little while. I'll probably sleep for a while, and I will let you know when I'm feeling better." This approach seemed to work a lot better than lashing out and yelling at them.

Above all else—and this is the reason you are reading these words—I not only asked God to help me not waste any opportunity, but I also asked him to use my life, suffering, and story for his purposes—to help and inspire others. I wasn't even sure I would be able to step onto the Purdue campus in August, but little did I know at the time the absolutely unfathomable ways God was going to answer my request.

CHAPTER 17

Defining Moments

(Tony & Kelly)

After the initial shock of the news began to somewhat lessen, something in Tyler was obviously different this time. While it was certainly devastating for all of us, he seemed to take it better than we did.

We worried that the darkness and despair that tried to destroy him the first time might consume him again, but as time went on, Tyler refused to give in to it. He had once told us during a particularly low moment of his first bout that if the cancer ever were to come back, he was not going to go through chemo again. "Never again" was his general attitude back then.

But this time, somehow, he was a different Tyler.

He talked about his disappointment with the way he had handled his first experience with cancer. He felt like he had wasted some opportunities during the first experience to do some good with the bad hand he had been dealt.

This was perhaps the defining moment of his life. He intentionally committed his uncertain future—which now certainly included cancer—to the Lord. It was inspiring. He asked God to use it in whatever way he might see fit. We didn't know it at the time, but God was more than just listening to his prayer—God was ready to open up the floodgates. He gave Tyler platform after platform and situation after situation wherein his prayer would be answered.

In this moment, Tyler taught us something. We became students of his who were about to be exposed to a level of an inner courage and strength that Tyler had in Christ beyond what we knew existed. It wasn't what we were asking; we were asking for healing and to avoid going through this hell with our child again. Tyler was asking for healing as well, but he put this other request first—and doing so started a chain reaction that has affected millions of lives in ways none of us could have ever fathomed.

So as we started down the next road of surgeries, genomic chemotherapy, and the like, we did so with a different kid under our care— a young man who was ready to forge a different path, regardless of what blocked his way. He was driven by a desire to be used by God and to keep living life to the fullest.

From a practical standpoint, nothing about his drive to live fully was more important to him than starting college that August. He didn't care what happened; he was going to school, no matter what. He knew he wasn't normal, but he wanted to be in a normal situation as much as possible. He had dreams of being on campus, being with friends, and going to sporting events where he could paint his body and scream like a maniac.

We decided we would not be the ones to hold him back from chasing these experiences, like attending college or being involved in various activities on campus, even though our first parental inclination was to lock him away in a bubble to keep him safe and hopefully extend his life. We realized that the illusion that we could keep our children completely safe was not real.

We had our doubts. We had anger. But God never rejected us, even when we questioned him. He kept giving us grace. He kept offering us peace, if only enough for one moment at a time.

Many people want to ask the question "Why?" when they face moments like these. We've asked it many times. But through many difficult moments, we came to the conclusion that we will never fully find the answer to "Why?" So we decided to ask a different question: "Who?"

It is God who is the giver of life. He did not originate the suffering in this world; the sin of humankind and the deception of Satan, the enemy of our souls, did. Yet God decided to not leave us alone to face all this suffering. He came and suffered with us. He knew what it felt like to hurt as much as we were hurting—and he is still in the process of redeeming all things so that one day there truly will be no more cancer or death.

But for now, we're waiting—and we're trusting in the "who," even if he were to allow one of our earthly lives to end sooner than we want. We know there is a place more real and lasting than where we are now. It's been hard, but we keep finding strength outside of ourselves to trust. Even when we don't trust very well, he keeps giving us grace anyway.

Tyler was always a gift, so we put our energies into trusting the one who gave him to us in the first place, even if he were to allow cancer to return . . . even if he might let him be taken away from us someday.

Statistically, when cancer returns, the odds of a good outcome decline considerably. Even so, we knew we had gifted surgeons and doctors at Riley. There were multiple treatment strategies available to try this time, so we had good reasons to hope. With God's help, we could beat this, so we just continued to try to live life and to have faith. We continued to believe.

Tyler started chemotherapy in April 2017, but we knew he would also need a hip-replacement surgery as well. All this threatened to disrupt his plans to be able to start school at Purdue in August. Also, the treatment path at that point was not cut and dry. There were multiple ways it could go down, which yet again made all of us nervous about his ability to start school on time.

After multiple rounds of chemo, we scheduled another MRI to determine if he was ready for the surgery. Tyler's oncologist was adamant about getting the tumor out of his body as soon as possible, which made a lot of sense. The longer the tumor was inside, the greater the odds that it would continue to grow, or even spread to other areas.

But Tyler's surgeon overruled his oncologist, opting to put off the surgery as long as possible to let the tumor decrease in size. The chemo seemed to be working according to the activity-level scale they used to measure growth or diminishment. On a scale of one to fifteen, it was now at two. When Tyler first began treatment, it was at eleven. This gave the surgeon more confidence to wait, with the hopes that they could almost completely kill off the tumor before surgery.

This would make the surgery a lot less intensive because they wouldn't have to cut as many bones. It also meant they could possibly scrape some of the tumor off of his bone instead of cutting it out of the bone, which would also lessen the invasiveness and speed up his subsequent recovery. We could definitely see where the surgeon was coming from, so we agreed to continue with two more twenty-one-day precision genomic treatment cycles, followed by additional scans to determine if the time for surgery was now ideal.

Looking at the calendar, there was a good chance that the surgery could be as late as the middle of the fall semester, or as early as several days before school. According to the surgeon, the rehab time would depend upon how Tyler's body responded to the operation. So we just held our breath, trusted God, and decided to ride this crazy ride.

We reached out to Purdue and communicated what was going on. Their response to our situation was absolutely incredible, as it has been ever since. They promised to help in any way they could. That included allowing Tyler to make up work as needed, including tests, projects, and the like. Considering his situation, they also agreed to amend the absentee policy for him, if at any time he needed such for medical reasons. It was so evident that Purdue was definitely where he belonged. As time passed, they continued to prove this to us over and over again. God's fingerprints were all over this process . . . Purdue was a reflection of divine love to us.

Tyler registered for twelve hours of classes, a full-time class load. The only change he made due to his situation was to trade physical education for philosophy. He planned to pick up the credit during a future semester.

As Tyler began treatment, we learned that the large quantities of chemotherapy he had been taking for so long were beginning to take a negative toll on his body. This led the doctors to temporarily discontinue any traditional chemo and put him exclusively on precision genomic treatments. They said his liver would soon be at the brink of failure if we continued with any more of these traditional treatments.

Just like his friend, Angelo Wilford, who had died from similar issues, Tyler was facing the complications of having received too much chemotherapy over a lifetime. Many cancer patients face the possibility of organ failure due to the toxic chemicals being pumped into their bodies, even though without these chemicals, they will surely die much quicker. It is a tragically delicate balance.

So Tyler continued with the genomics, but since the overall chemo plan had now changed, the surgeon called us in early August and asked if we would want to do the surgery the next week. Tyler said yes.

Within ten days of having a hip replacement, he limped onto the Purdue campus. They had no idea what was about to hit them.

Tyler sitting on his momma's lap as we
celebrate his 4th birthday.

Ethan, Blake, and Tyler riding their razor
scooters on the Monon Trail in our home
town of Carmel, Indiana.

Family Christmas card picture, 2010.

Tyler, Blake, and Ethan (Thing 1, 2, and
3), on our family vacation in Florida.

Tyler loving on Blake, one of his brothers.

The boys! Blake, Tyler, and Ethan, fall of
2016.

Tyler riding a dolphin during our Make A
Wish trip to Hawaii in January 2016.

The Crull, Campbell, and Trent
Christmas, 2017.

Grandma and Grandpa Campbell on the beach with Tyler in Gulf Shores over spring break 2015.

Tyler with our senior pastor, Mark Vroegop.

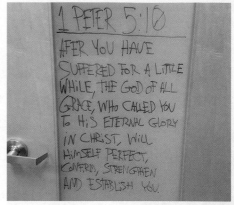

Tyler wrote this scripture on his hospital door during his cancer treatment (1 Peter 5:10).

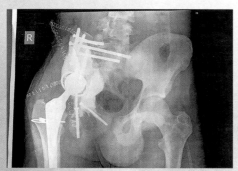

X-ray of Tyler's prostectic hip after his hip-replacement surgery. Ten days after surgery, Tyler limped onto the Purdue campus.

Tyler's first day at Purdue University.

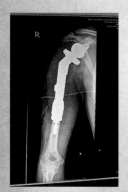

X-ray of Tyler's prostectic arm after his reverse-shoulder surgery.

The Trent family celebrating Christmas in 2018.

Photo courtesy of Purdue University

Tyler having fun rooting on his favorite Purdue Boilermakers his freshman year at a basketball game.

Tyler traveling to Chicago for the parade to celebrate the Cubs winning the 2016 World Series.

Tyler during one of his chemo infusions with that smile of his!

Our family visiting the Indianapolis Colts' complex on the last day of spring training and meeting quarterback Andrew Luck.

Tyler and one of his childhood best buds, Josh Seals, camping out before the first Purdue football home game in 2017. This game signifies the begining of the #TylerStrong™ movement.

Tyler and Ethan getting a surprise, special home visit from the Indianapolis Colts mascot, Blue.

Our family, along with Grandma Campbell, celebrating the big Purdue win over Ohio State!

Tyler speaking at the Purdue University Dance Marathon for Riley Children's hospital his freshman year (fall of 2017).

Tyler and his youth group leaders and friends, who shaved their heads in honor and support of his first diagnosis in summer of 2014, praying for him.

Tyler on high school graduation day.

Tyler's high school graduation party, where his cousins and brother surprised him by shaving their heads in honor of Tyler and his Grandpa Campbell, who was also fighting cancer.

Tyler sharing his story and encouraging others to join the fight to raise money for pediatric cancer at the Miracle Network Dance Marathon Leadership Conference.

Tyler being interviewed by sportscaster Scott Van Pelt on his T.V. show, *SportsCenter with Scott Van Pelt*

Tyler surrounded in support by his PUDM friends at the Miracle Network Dance Marathon Leadership Conference.

Family and pastors praying over Tyler before surgery to remove the tumor, replace his right hip, and reconstruct his pelvis (July 2017).

Dear friend Gregg Doyel showing love to Tyler the way he always did, by gently placing his head on Tyler's as a manner of embrace.

Tyler's beloved high school youth pastor and dear friend, Joe Wittmer, during one of his many visits.

Two of our pastors, Don Bartemus and Joe Wittmer, before one of Tyler's many surgeries.

Dear friend Trey Mock, Blue Mascot for the Indianapolis Colts. This picture was taken while in Nashville for the Music City Bowl where Trey accompanied us and helped us care for Tyler.

Three of Tyler's dearest, oldest friends: Anni Osborne, Jake Heinzman, and Noah Osborne.

Special visit from Indianapolis Colts kicker, Adam Vinatieri, bringing Tyler the gift of a Drew Brees signed jersey.

"We are shaped by our experiences, and we are the people that we are, because of the things we've been through."

Photo courtesy of Purdue University

Photo courtesy of Purdue University

Purdue football captains visiting Tyler the day after beating Nebraska and presenting him with the game ball.

Dr. Gary R. Bertoline, Dean of the Purdue Polytechnic Institute, personally delivering Tyler's degree in computer information technology.

On our way to the Music City Bowl in Nashville thanks to Indianapolis Colts' owner Jim Irsay, who let us borrow his private plane (December 28, 2018).

Photo courtesy of Purdue University

In the locker room with Coach Brohm and QB David Blough after Purdue beat IU.

On the Purdue football field freshman year as honorary captain with Ja'Whaun Bently for the Hammer Down Cancer game.

On our way to the Music City Bowl game in Nashville (December 28, 2018).

Tyler's Purdue roommates and friends at a 2018 football game holding up the flag they had made in his honor.

Photo courtesy of Purdue University

In Nashville for the Music City Bowl. Tyler was on the field as the honorary captain with his dad and QB David Blough (December 28, 2018).

Photo by Phil Ellsworth/ESPN Images

Tyler receiving the Disney Spirit Award at the Home Depot College Football awards in Atlanta on December 6, 2018. Reporter Tom Rinaldi, from ESPN and College Game Day, presented Tyler with the award; he was joined onstage by Purdue QB David Blough.

Tyler receiving the Patrick Mackey Courage Award at the National Football Foundation of Northwest Indiana in June 2018.

Tyler, at the Riley Foundation Be the Hope NOW luncheon, receiving the Sagamore of the Wabash award from Indiana Governor Eric Holcomb. It is the highest civilian award given in the state of Indiana (November 28, 2018).

While in Atlanta for the Home Depot College Football Awards, visiting Turner Studios and the set of *Inside the NBA* with hosts Ernie Johnson, Charles Barkley, Kenny Smith, and Shaquille O'Neal.

Tyler, Ethan, and Blake at the luncheon for the Music City Bowl in Nashville (December 27, 2018).

Tyler with his Disney Spirit award after receiving it in the mail.

CHAPTER 18

Limping In, Camping Out, and Speaking Up

(Tyler)

I went under the knife again, which is never fun. But all told, my hip replacement was a success . . . just another major surgery stamp to add to my medical passport.

Limping into My Freshman Year

While recovery had its low moments, I tried to begin walking as soon as possible on crutches, to speed up the recovery process. With all those prayers about starting school on time in my rearview mirror, about ten days after my hip replacement, this new college freshman—limping on crutches, mind you—actually *walked* to my first class at Purdue University. God had come through for me yet again.

I probably had one of the more unique freshman situations. I was receiving chemo treatments in what felt like a parallel universe—the one where I had cancer. Then back in the real world, I was going to class like any other college kid. So how did my life work in these parallel universes of cancer and college?

It began with mobility. I couldn't walk normally, but at least I was walking. I slept way more than I ever expected. I guess in this way, I was a pretty stereotypical college student because I could slumber right on through a tornado. The only difference was that I hadn't been up partying until 3:00 a.m. the night before.

Well, *usually* I hadn't. (Just kidding, Mom.)

Purdue offered me the opportunity to bypass the normal rules for freshmen and live in a single room rather than having to share a room with a roommate. Let's be honest, most anyone who has ever attended college for any amount of time at all has a roommate horror story. So to most people I knew, I was being offered the golden ticket. But I declined.

More than a few of my friends thought I was a little bit crazy when I turned down this generous offer in favor of a normal freshman rooming situation instead—complete with roommate. Life was about relationships. And I wanted to be around people. Very quickly, I made some of my best friends at school, guys like my roommate John Kruse, Kyle Gurjal, Sam Booth, and Collin Marmeyer.

Avoiding the isolation of being in a single room was one of the single best decisions I ever made. The friendships I made on the main floor of Tarkington Hall proved to be the most integral component of the college experience that, for so many years, I had wanted so desperately to have. Because of these guys, I experienced everything I had hoped for—and then some. The friendship, fun, and crazy camaraderie we forged together in those filthy dorm rooms exceeded my wildest expectations, fostering memories that will outlast my time on this earth, no matter how long or short it may be.

My typical morning on campus was probably pretty similar to any other freshman's morning. I would wake up at 6:00 a.m. and hit the showers, which were located in one of the most disgusting bathrooms on Earth. But I loved even the less-than-plush restrooms at Tarkington Hall. They were just another fun part of my college experience.

After this, depending on the morning, I was off to my first class. Often, this meant sitting down to a mental breakfast of Math 161: Calculus 1, also technically known as Plain Analytical Geometry. It was a pretty fun class with a professor who had a great sense of humor, which made the process of learning more entertaining.

But this is where my campus experience would begin to cross into atypical territory. Depending on the week, after class I would get into my car to drive back to my house in Carmel to meet my mom and ride together to Riley Children's Hospital. Sometimes, I would get updated scans to check the progress of my treatment. This was usually followed by a trip to the oncology clinic for blood work, followed by four or five days of precision genomic chemotherapy. I would often do my coursework from my hospital bed.

The hardest part about my first semester at Purdue was twofold: maintaining my stamina, and navigating the campus on crutches. From a stamina standpoint, I just had to sleep when I couldn't go anymore. From a navigation standpoint, I just had to keep going. I had the blessing of being able to drive to class, but I still had to make my way from building to building, and then upstairs and downstairs, depending on where the class was held.

You have to remember that from day one, I was in the process of "breaking in" my newly constructed artificial hip, so to speak. (It's probably never a good thing to use the words "break" and "hip" in the same sentence.) My new hip would still require a follow-up surgery a few months later, over Christmas break. This meant I couldn't put my full weight on my left foot, which made walking long distances less than ideal. Even so, I managed to get around okay. I was just grateful to be able to go to school at all.

In addition to all the things normal and abnormal about my life in school, crazy things outside my health crisis were beginning to take shape—hidden things related to my life's purpose and legacy that God began to unwrap in unexpected and remarkable ways.

Camping Out

Amid the ups and downs of the seesaw that was my life, something else began to happen that seemingly made no sense at all: my story began to be known.

Many people have asked me, "Why you? There are so many people out there with cancer, so why is your story being talked about all over ESPN and by millions on social media?" It's a fair question. I certainly don't have an exceptional story, though I think it is unique. What I mean is, I haven't climbed Everest, created a billion-dollar industry out of my college dorm room, or invented a new microchip for the space shuttle.

When you really break it down, I'm just a dude . . . a dude with cancer.

However, it was at this moment in my story that the answer to the question of my unlikely notoriety began to take shape. For me, it always goes back to that simple prayer I offered up when I was diagnosed for the second time, asking God to use my story and suffering for something higher and bigger than myself. I asked him to help me not waste any opportunity in my life, including cancer.

If you're reading these words, then you are a part of God's answer to that prayer. But when I prayed it, I had no idea that his answer would include all the incredible things that have happened to me—or that it would include you. Back then, I just wanted it all to matter. I didn't ask for fame and could have never expected it in a hundred years.

I didn't ask for my story to be heard because I already knew I had everything I needed, having been made in God's image and being deeply loved by him. No, I desired that my life would simply be counted among those who have the honor of pointing many others to a hope higher than the suffering of this world. God heard and answered my request in ways that were "immeasurably more than all we ask or imagine, according to his power that is at work within us" (Ephesians 3:20, NIV).

This crazy part of my story really began with another miracle of sorts: the Purdue football team actually began to win games. Over the previous four years, we had a dismal record of nine wins and thirty-nine losses—nothing to write home about, much less write good sports articles about.

But when we opened up the season against a strong Louisville squad in 2017, we suddenly looked like a different team. We lost the game, but only by a single touchdown. We then turned around and won the next game against the University of Ohio, followed by a blowout win against SEC opponent Missouri. We were sitting at 2–1 heading into a home matchup against the top-ten ranked Michigan Wolverines, who were undefeated.

Now, I had decided that if I was going to attend Purdue, I was going to go "all in" on being a Purdue sports enthusiast. If I truly am the Purdue "super-fan," whatever that means, I guess you could say this was a key moment in my superhero backstory, though I'm not sure how heroic it was. It was pretty simple: I wanted to go all out for our game against Michigan to generate excitement and momentum for the Boilermakers among the student body and the fans.

Yes, we were underdogs, but this was a role I knew well—it didn't have to stop us from giving our friends in the football program a little boost of encouragement, and our opponents coming to town a little dose of intimidation, something most schools playing Purdue at home had not felt since Drew Brees was throwing the ball. I wanted to change that. I wanted to help energize the fan base. Besides, the Big Ten Network was going to be broadcasting their pregame program from West Lafayette, so it was a perfect chance to churn up some excitement.

I knew I couldn't do this alone—enter, as usual, my best friend, Josh Seals. We decided to do our favorite thing: put our goofy heads together and see what manner of goofiness resulted from it. The brilliant idea that resulted from our epic meeting of the minds was to set up camp outside the stadium the night before the game to be the first ones in line the next morning when they opened the gate for students. At that time in the sad tale that was Purdue football, no one—and I mean, *no one*—camped out for tickets.

We set out to change that.

It was obviously a Friday, but not just any Friday. It was one of those Fridays when I had to undergo a round of chemotherapy earlier in the day. After I left the hospital, I swung by my house to meet Josh—we lived in the same neighborhood—and to pick up our gear. He brought along his tent and air mattress. And so we were off to Purdue to camp out alone for tickets that no one else wanted.

We set up our little campsite and wore our best black and gold, but I took it one step further, donning a vertical-striped pair of Purdue overalls—and of course, going shirtless underneath. It was all class, with just a slight hint of redneck—and really hot.

But then there was the matter of promotion. All the "cool kids" at the time were setting up new Twitter accounts, and I had just joined their ranks. So I took a picture of Josh and me in the tent outside Ross-Ade Stadium and tweeted it at the Boilermaker football account.

That little tweet produced some pretty massive results.

The Boilermakers account retweeted my post to their thousands of followers. Next thing we knew, we noticed a few people walking toward our tent. We thought it was campus safety and figured we were in trouble. But they were local reporters, just intrigued by what we were doing. This was one of the first times I was interviewed by the local media, but it would not be the last.

We had a few more visitors and then eventually went to sleep for the night. The next morning, another visitor showed up bright and early: Coach Jeff Brohm, the head coach of the Purdue football team. He was so grateful for our support of the program and wanted to personally thank us.

I was dumbfounded that he showed up. It was almost unthinkable that a head coach would take time out of his morning on game day—time that he could have been using to prep for the game—just to say thank you to a couple of college kids who had made the silly decision to sleep on concrete for twelve hours before a football game. But this was just the level of character I would continue to see in Coach Brohm. He was kind to me in a way that changed the course of my very story.

My parents, showing concern for me, questioned the wisdom of sleeping on concrete (on an air mattress, obviously) after just receiving six hours of chemotherapy. It does kind of call my SAT scores into question, or at least the critical-thinking section of the exam. I was indeed tired, and there was no doubt that a difficult road lay ahead of me, but this was simply something I would have done whether or not I was sick.

Coach Brohm told me that he was going to share what we had done with the team before the game to encourage them. Little did I know that this initial connection would begin a close relationship with him and with the players—a connection that would allow me the honor of supporting and encouraging them many times over in the future. Little did I know all the ways they would support and encourage me in return.

When it was all said and done, our experience of camping out at the stadium was really the first time my story began to get picked up by local and regional media outlets. It seemed pretty odd to me at the time—I had no idea what God was up to.

Stories about me—a Purdue student and crazed fan with cancer—began popping up here and there in various newspapers and on various news stations. I sort of figured my story would be a "flash in the pan," but for some reason, the flames kept getting bigger and bigger. Sometimes I sit on my bed and do a Google search for my name—not to be narcissistic or self-centered, but simply to marvel at what God has done with my story. The search result is overwhelming—how could so many things be written about someone like me? It is truly humbling.

I only wish there were articles written about every person who has ever written about me because everyone has a story that needs to be heard.

Some of those reporters would become dear friends to me, especially Gregg Doyel from the *IndyStar*. A hilarious guy and a brilliant writer, he spent more hours in my house just hanging out than I could ever count. His realness and authenticity have affected me deeply. There's just something about someone who is in it for more than himself—who is okay with not being the center of the universe. That was Gregg Doyel, along with many others I met along the way.

I can't explain the momentum that began building. From the stories that circulated about us camping out to more interactions with the football team, it felt like a new opportunity happened every day. Soon, I was also being asked to share my story with various small groups, church groups, athletic teams, and other organizations on campus.

Sharing my story with live groups (as opposed to having the media share my story) began as most important things do—with a friend. In this case, I had made a new friend, and we had been having some incredible discussions after reading through certain scriptures together. Through our time together, he learned all about my story—including my first bout with cancer, the doubt and darkness that almost killed me at my own hand, and the new battle I was facing at this very moment. He happened to be one of the leaders of a CRU (a Christian organization on campus) Bible study that was meeting on our residence hall floor. He asked me to share my story—and my faith—with the other guys on our floor.

He personally went door to door on our floor and invited everyone to come, whether they were a believer or not. There was no pressure and no judgment. I was so excited to get to share the hope I had found through the life I was still figuring out every day with Christ. I just wanted to share with anyone who would listen—and many showed up to listen. They asked me a lot of follow-up questions, both in the moment and in the time that passed afterward.

Over the next year, I was invited many times to share my story and the hope I had found in Christ to numerous groups on Purdue's campus, including the volleyball team, softball team, baseball team, and obviously, the football team.

Someone once told me that I was like the unofficial Purdue mascot—everyone just seemed to know who I was. I think the truth is, God just flipped a switch and decided to use my life for something bigger than myself. I could tell he was directing my path in these opportunities, even as the path of my health was still so uncertain. Yes, I wanted him to direct that path as well toward the outcome I most desired—healing. But I must tell you, the fact that he was using my life to encourage, inspire, and lift up other people—no matter how long this life might last—was the most incredibly fulfilling thing I've ever experienced.

Maybe that's why David said that the love of God is "better than life" (Psalm 63:3, NIV).

My life's very status was in question, but it truly felt that I was experiencing something better as I lived out a daily story higher than anything I could have ever drawn up as a life plan on this earth. It felt as if I was living life to the fullest.

It was grace, plain and simple.

Speaking Up

Another key development during my freshman year was going to work as a sports beat writer for the *Purdue Exponent*, Purdue's campus newspaper. This was one of the great joys of my life, affording me the opportunity to really live and breathe as a writer in my element—sports statistics and reporting. I also think this played greatly into my future connections with certain people in the media.

As a writer, even though I wasn't on the field or in the gymnasium as an athlete, I became every bit as much a "gym rat" as the players themselves. I took to the craft of interviewing and writing very easily, loving the whole process from start to finish. This also contributed to my connection with so many people on campus; I was constantly showing up to interview them for a story.

Try to picture it: I was walking on one crutch, coming and going from chemo treatments, and showing up for football practices, player and coach interviews, and of course, games. It's no wonder that along the way, I began to really get to know a lot of the players, and especially on the football team—I stood out.

The Purdue football team would teach me so much about brotherhood—about standing strong with someone no matter what weakness they may be facing. In the beginning, they obviously knew all about my situation because of the local media stories, so they were careful to never treat me like I was just a cancer patient; they treated me like a reporter. Besides brief and thoughtful check-ins here and there off the record, especially after we had gotten to know each other better, they never brought up my cancer during a professional interview. I was there to do a job, and I would like to think that I did it pretty well.

Again, my mantra was that everyone has a story to tell . . . there just has to be someone willing to listen to it. I think I picked up the idea from a high school worldview class. We learned about the ways that people look at life and the world through a variety of lenses. I didn't want my cancer to be the only lens through which they could see me. I wanted to blend—to be a purveyor of stories other than my own, something I believed would make the world a much better place if more people would try.

This is probably why being a sports writer came so naturally to me: I got to listen to other people's stories. Working for the newspaper became important to me, so much so that I hoped to do it for a living someday. Writing for the *Exponent* was the ultimate opportunity to "nerd out" on the stats and storylines, but for legitimate reasons. I even got to travel to New York to cover the Big Ten Basketball Tournament at Madison Square Garden, an experience that will stay with me forever.

On football game days, I was usually in the press box. I would write a story before the game that previewed the teams and highlight-ed portions of the pregame interviews with the players and coaches. I would usually then post something during halftime that updated the online readers and fans about the progress and status of the game. And of course, I would write post-game articles.

It was a pretty major time commitment, more than most people probably realize when they quickly click on a sports article about their favorite team. Even so, the experience was simply unparalleled, one of the best of my life.

I felt at home in this craft of writing, but I also felt at home shar-ing my story and hope with people. As my story gained more mo-mentum, more opportunities arose for me to talk about it publicly, but there was a special place in my heart for other cancer patients, especially children.

Riley Children's was a place where I made so many friends, but it was the kids who really stole my heart—and never gave it back. At times, there were kids there whose parents were also sick and couldn't care for them. There were also kids who didn't have parents at all for one reason or another. I sometimes witnessed parents dropping off their children at the beginning of a chemo treatment cycle, then coming back to pick them up at the end. I'm sure they felt they had no choice in light of their work commitments conflicting with their kids' treatment times—and considering the kind of financial burden it is to have a chronically sick child, this was often the best they could do under the circumstances.

Regardless, it broke my heart that kids would have to go through any stage of this horrific journey through cancer alone—even for a second. I know I was very blessed in my situation to have loving par-ents and a family who were able to stay with me through everything I faced, including overnight stays. If you've never slept in a hospital room that is not your own, you don't know what you're missing . . . and you should be thankful, as should your back. Those chairs are rock hard.

I began to encounter kids who were not as fortunate as me. Some of them came from broken homes and complicated family situations. I knew God had uniquely positioned me to be able to spend time with them, sharing fun, hope, and the love of Christ with them. I kept asking God to take my story into the most vulnerable situations. It would be difficult to find another area in which he answered my prayer so directly and joyfully as my time with these precious children.

I also had significant conversations with the doctors and nurses, who were already saints in my book, but who had struggles of their own to face. One of my main doctors was not a believer (a follower of Jesus Christ). He began asking me questions about our family and about the joy we seemed to have under such dire circumstances. I was able to share my ultimate hope with him.

Opportunities surrounded me, even as cancer tried to annihilate me.

The administration at Riley was always kind to me, so I always tried to do my best to partner with them in helping others. Once we all began to see that my story was curiously gaining significant exposure in the community, we began to figure out ways that this development might be an opportunity to raise awareness and funds for cancer research.

One of the main fund-raising efforts of Riley is the Purdue University Dance Marathon (PUDM). This is a yearlong movement dedicated to enhancing the lives of children with cancer. Their goal is to provide emotional and financial support for the families of kids at Riley by raising funds for cancer research at the Herman B. Wells Pediatric Research Center and by helping to financially support the Child Life Zone within the hospital. Their efforts culminate every year in an eighteen-hour, no-sitting, no-sleeping Dance Marathon.

You may have never heard of it, but this event is a huge deal, with hundreds of dance teams mobilizing to raise funds for cancer research. It really taps into the Purdue student population, helping them step up as leaders in this fight. I knew I wanted to be at the front lines of this war, so imagine my delight when Riley asked me to share my story and my faith at the PUDM event.

That was one of the most enjoyable and most defining moments of my life. All my friends from Tarkington Hall joined me in raising more than $100,000 for cancer research at PUDM. Around the same time, I was also asked to sit on the board of the Purdue Center For Cancer Research, an honor never before bestowed on a student. I was floored, even as God was being lifted up higher and higher.

I'm happy to boast in what God has done through the tireless work of my friends at Riley and at Purdue. Looking back, it's hard to imagine that over the course of the first year of my college career, I stood before thousands of people on a nonreligious university campus and at a nonreligious medical facility and was asked to unapologetically and freely share not only about my journey through cancer, but also about the hope I had found in Christ.

I may have limped into college, but God was letting me stand tall in a grace that surpassed any expectations I could have ever imagined.

CHAPTER 19

The Third Time's No Charm

(Tyler)

Sometime in early February 2018, during the second semester of my freshman year, I began experiencing severe back pain. It was not unusual for me to experience random pains of many kinds on a daily basis. I would compare it to what I would imagine elderly people might experience—chronic pain.

But I was just nineteen.

This pain in my back was more severe than usual. At first, I told myself to give it a couple of days to subside, like any other random pain I might feel. It wasn't uncommon for some sort of new pain to flare up for a day or two, but it was uncommon for it not to fade away in forty-eight hours or so.

But this pain became so bad that I could no longer sleep. We went to meet with one of my doctors about it, hoping it was nothing more than a minor twinge related to my pelvis—perhaps pain emanating to my back because of general soreness or a lack of alignment in my hip area.

Once again, I was back in the hospital for an X-ray. Once again, the X-ray came back looking pretty good, at least concerning my pelvis. In fact, they were pretty surprised at how well my pelvis was healing. Everything looked stable, and my hipbone was growing back as it should. But unfortunately, this did not explain my back pain.

Sometimes, the strange thing about medical diagnoses is that good news can be bad news when it doesn't offer a good explanation for a persistent symptom. You are grateful for good news on one front, but the mystery remaining on the other end is still unresolved.

Back . . . Again

So once again, I underwent that dreaded MRI. To scan my back, they obviously wanted me to lie flat on my back, but I couldn't do so because the pain was so excruciatingly severe. I could not physically do it, even though I wanted to.

The medical staff suggested that we reschedule the MRI for a bit later so that I could have time to take pain medication beforehand to help with the process of lying flat. A week later, my mom drove me to the hospital for the second attempt at the MRI. But even then, the pain just cut right through the meds like a hot knife through butter. I simply could not lie there for the duration of the test, even though I would like to think that I had developed a pretty high pain tolerance by then.

The next step was to put me to sleep to perform the MRI, so another week later, that's what we did. The MRI revealed what appeared to be a pocket of liquid near the L4 and L3 area of my spine. Their initial thought was that some sort of infection had set up in the area, probably materializing back when my white blood cell counts were really low. That would explain why my body had not been able to fight it off. They wanted to go in and drain (aspirate) it to relieve the pressure and to figure out exactly what was going on.

This meant yet another surgery, which tragically, had become far too familiar. So I went under the knife again. When they got into the area, they discovered that the pocket was actually a blood clot that had possibly formed during the healing process after I had unknowingly torn a muscle. They were able to successfully aspirate the blood clot, and because they were in there already, they decided to retrieve a sample of some of the blood for testing. They also scraped some of the bone off my spine. These were all precautionary measures as a result of my history; they just wanted to make sure everything around the area of the blood clot was also looking good as well.

After testing and evaluating all the data together, they finally discovered a three-centimeter osteosarcoma tumor essentially hanging out near the L4 area of my spine.

Once again, I had developed cancer in a new location . . . for a third time.

As you know by now, the discovery of cancer leads to a frantic flurry of activity to quickly ascertain the best course of action. After all, and especially as mine had proven to us time and time again, cancer can grow very, very fast. We knew that the more time it had to grow, the more it would continue to intrude into my nerve head, which would eventually cause me to lose function in my right leg. Furthermore, the larger it would grow, the harder it would be to remove without damaging my spinal cord. A wrong move could lead to paralysis.

It's difficult to describe the way I felt after this third diagnosis. I would say that my first reaction was confusion because I had been undergoing constant chemotherapy since December of the previous year. It was now mid-March. Chemo was seemingly killing the tumor on my pelvis, so in my mind, intuitive logic would assume that cancer could not be simultaneously growing elsewhere, even though chemo is not necessarily a preventive treatment. It was just an assumption, I suppose—or perhaps a hope.

The moment the news came, I was leaving for New York to cover the Big Ten Basketball Tournament for the *Purdue Exponent*, an independent school newspaper. My parents already had the news, but they didn't tell me until I returned a few days later. They didn't want to ruin my experience; and to be honest, I'm grateful that they didn't.

By the time they told me, my brothers, Blake and Ethan, already knew. I could tell it was very hard on them this time—they had already lived for so long in the shadow of my cancer diagnosis. They cared so much about me, and I hated so much the idea of putting them through even more pain and trouble.

My brothers were the best two reasons I had to stay strong in my attitude and in my faith in Christ's bigger plan for my life. They were experiencing this, too. I could tell—or at least I hope—that the way I handled moments like these helped them deal with the gravity of our family's situation. I'm not saying it made it *easy* on them, but I do hope that in the moments when I didn't lose heart, it at least made it *easier*. I was the oldest. I had to set a good example for them.

At that time, I was only two months away from being done with treatments, so there was a fairly strong sense of emotional confusion as well. I was close, or so I had thought. But now I was suddenly so very far away. I guess I had a slight sense of security before, knowing that we were treating my cancer aggressively and that it appeared to be responding.

But now, we all returned again to living in the land of uncertainty.

Even so, in terms of my faith, I never dive-bombed back into the darkness the way I did after the first diagnosis. God's love had become so undeniably real to me that there was no going back to a place of wondering if his intentions toward me were good or bad, even though I had no idea what moving forward would look like.

I had come to truly believe that I was going through this for a reason . . . for something much more real than just cancer. God had used my circumstances to build a pretty solid platform from which I had been able to share hope and help with all kinds of people.

Even so, the question of why was still there. I didn't like the fact that God had allowed this, even though I trusted his ultimate intention and plan. But in my mind and in my hypothetical plans, it seemed to make perfect sense that all the good I was being a part of would continue for years to come, if not for the rest of my long life. This way, more good could be done for more people. The incredible opportunities coming my way seemed to be ramping up, not tapering off. I also felt that I had handled myself fairly well in the process, learning more about my shortcomings and weaknesses, while also being more honest with God and others as I lived out my story.

I guess what I'm saying is that it seemed like the Lord could have taken all this to a really cool place other than a third cancer diagnosis and all the uncertainty it brought along with it. It definitely felt like a setback, if for no other reason than it brought back the realization that all this might not last as long as I had originally hoped.

Yes, I had serious questions and doubts, but thankfully, there were anchors in my life—anchors that had already proven trustworthy. So I decided to tie off to them again. My family. My friends. My faith—

and the stunning realization hidden from most people in the plain sight of suffering that real faith is not at all the absence of questions, disappointment, or even anger.

Real faith is honest, so it never requires a mask or a facade. It might be blurry, but it is never blind. Faith simply chooses to see the object of trust as a *someone* whose love has become a certainty rather than merely the *something* that is causing the uncertainty in the first place. I did not like this turn in my story, but I had discovered that putting my ultimate hope in an outcome was a slippery slope upon which no one could stand.

I still had intense moments of weakness, but I had also grown into a place of belief. I had become intimately and painfully aware of my weakness, which helped me to finally give up and trust in the strength of another instead. No strength in myself was required. None.

I had a whole bucket of unbelief, which I think is natural, but Christ had made it where even this couldn't prevent me from believing him if I still wanted to choose to do so. Jesus had covered every base here, even the doubt and uncertainty that most people assume negates their ability to "have faith."

I had learned that my very ability to believe was also a gift from Jesus offered to all people. Trusting him did not first require a mastery of my doubts; I could also trust him with the very things that seemingly keep me from trusting him. Every barrier has been removed in the death and resurrection of Jesus. As the desperate father of a severely sick and tormented child once told Jesus, "I believe; help my unbelief!"

He did—and that's what he did with me, too.

Cancer, a Formidable Opponent

I had definitely grown in my trust, but I still faced an extremely difficult challenge ahead. My heart was not the only thing growing and thriving; so too was the cancer in my body.

As we met with my doctors over the days that followed, it became apparent that my cancer was pretty intelligent—that is, it had the uncanny ability to morph and evolve, no matter what chemotherapy we threw at it. I used to joke with my friends that my cancer was like an Advanced Placement-qualified, tier-one genius of a cancer. It had learned to keep adapting to survive, but unfortunately, my body was not proving able to do the same in response.

Even when various treatment paths were successful in "killing" the tumors in my arm and pelvis, they still couldn't keep the cancer from learning and growing in other areas. Our efforts worked to a certain degree, but the reality was setting in that my body simply did not have whatever thing it needed to fend off the onslaught of this particular cancer. Something in my body was different from the bodies of my friends and family—mine could not seem to win the fight against this formidable opponent.

Even so, my brilliant doctor friends on our medical team were relentless in trying to help me beat this. They never gave up. They kept looking for clinical trials and other options, which usually had about a 20 to 30 percent chance of working . . . the first time. These odds continued to weaken as we had already passed the second bout, now gearing up toward the third. It had seemingly worked with my pelvis, but there was no guarantee it would now work with my spine.

But the good news was that besides the back pain, I was not suffering from any other side effects of the tumor on my spine. I would sometimes jokingly tell people that besides the tumors in my body, I was perfectly healthy.

Considering the circumstances, I was fortunate and blessed to not be facing organ failure. This was especially true about my liver, which had processed and metabolized an incredible amount of chemotherapy over the years. My doctors told me that it probably should have shut down by that point, but surprisingly, it was functioning really well. This was good news, but at the same time, odds in the 20 or 30 percent range sound like failing grades to a straight-A student.

Finding Ways for My Cancer to Help Others

As my future became more uncertain, I began to grow more certain that this latest development wasn't all about me. I had met thousands of people—adults, children, and families—who were facing the horrors of their own cancer stories. In fact, after a few key conversations with my doctors, I began to learn that there were additional ways my cancer might help others.

These possibilities were related to my treatment options. We had used only two of the genomic options during my previous treatments, which meant there were around three more we could still try. Or we could go down the path of a clinical trial—that is, pursue treatment that no one had ever undergone before. The additional benefit of this option was how it might benefit other patients in the future.

If I were to do a clinical trial, it would produce completely new data that could be contributed to emerging cancer research. In this respect, the growth of my tumor—as horrible as it was—could be used for a worthy, possibly even life-saving cause. It would hopefully help other people down the road find access to better drugs and better treatment options.

When you first get cancer, everything in the world feels like it revolves around you. It's a reactionary survival instinct. But when I reached my third go-round, I was grateful that my situation might help affect others as well. Every single year, thousands of children are diagnosed with cancer—kids just like me. If there was a chance that I could help to even slow this trend in some form or fashion, I was willing to do anything, including going on a trial drug that might provide information for people down the road who would also face osteosarcoma.

I was no longer just a patient; I was a player in this game. I was no longer just a victim of cancer; I was an active fighter against it. I knew I could be a part of the upset of cancer, even if I wouldn't get to pull down the goalposts in my lifetime.

One of the coolest parts of this change of heart came when I was asked to donate a sample of two of my tumors for research purposes. Each tumor was given a name: TT1 and TT2, respectively. But we sometimes just would refer to them as T^2 (pronounced "T-squared"), which is the symbol I use for my signature, obviously standing for Tyler Trent. Of all the things I had ever hoped my name would be attached to, nothing made me prouder than this. My name would now be included in medical journals and among clinical research that would someday help another kid with osteosarcoma experience a cure and a cancer-free life.

I call that an upset for sure.

Into the Uncertainty

In the meantime, I had a spring semester of college classes to finish up. I knew I would probably have to drop at least one class due to the increased driving back and forth to Riley for chemo treatments. Purdue Center For Cancer Research also had multiple events coming up that I was supposed to be involved in. In addition to all of this, I was trying to lock down an internship for the summer doing sports analytics or research and development with a sports team that might be looking to hire freshmen interns.

I also signed up for online summer classes, specifically math, because it would be so much cheaper than on-campus options. I wanted to keep up with my hours but also gain enough credits to officially enter the major I wanted. I had completed twelve hours during my first semester, finishing with a 3.5 GPA. It kind of bugged me that I was a quarter point from making the Dean's List, but I suppose that's beside the point.

From a mobility standpoint, this diagnosis didn't pose any immediate problems, and I had no plans of slowing down. The real question, though, was whether or not we could get the tumor on my spine to stop growing. If this didn't happen, it was definitely going to eventually slow down my mobility.

And unfortunately, as the next few weeks and months passed, that is exactly what happened. The tumor did not respond to the treatments in the way we had hoped. This began to limit so much of what I wanted to do, both physically and mentally.

As the semester was coming to an end, I was offered the opportunity of a lifetime: a summer internship with BP Oil in Chicago. It was something that few people have the chance of experiencing, especially after just completing their freshman year. They wanted me to come work for their drone division, helping out with documents and data management. They would pay for my housing in Chicago, along with a hefty salary for three months of work—the kind of salary any college kid would drool over.

It was everything I had wanted, but I was struggling physically and mentally to get to it. I could tell I was getting worse, not better. It was happening quickly, yet it still felt like a slow, tortuous process. Eventually, I had to decline the BP Oil opportunity for health reasons. I can't even begin to explain how much that discouraged me. I was able to land a short summer opportunity working for the Indianapolis Colts organization, something for which I am eternally grateful, but I will always regret missing out on what might have been waiting for me in Chicago.

Searching Obsessively for a Solution

I began to sense that my doctors were running out of options. I know it wasn't their fault, but when you are the one facing your imminent mortality, you want everyone else to be as unreasonably tenacious in their efforts as you feel you are in your heart. In other words, I wanted them to manufacture a solution, but they simply could not.

At that point, I felt I just couldn't accept this as a reality. I began to feel that I was going to have to make something happen for myself. I became almost manic about finding a solution to this unending crisis. I wanted to go rogue, which is kind of what I did. I began to research every clinical trial and treatment out there. I was obsessed.

My dad joined in, frantically exploring every sort of radical, homeopathic, and nutritional possibility imaginable. For weeks on end, he would spend hours each day calling doctors all over the world, begging for options and answers. It was a hard time for both of us because, despite all our efforts, we just couldn't find the answers we were looking for. It caused a lot of friction in our family, which was already under a lot of pressure.

I hated that my situation contributed to everyone else's pressure, but I guess that's the price of being loved so well.

Still, I spent almost 70 percent of my spare time looking into various clinical trials in California and around the world, which was an all-consuming endeavor. There were so many medical documents and applications to pour over, requiring intense study and a lot of time to process. In terms of these trials, this one, that one, or the other one would look promising, but inevitably, something about my particular cancer or situation would keep me from being an eligible candidate.

The biggest deterrent to my qualification for these trials was the location of my tumor. There was a fear that the treatment would cause inflammation and possibly enlarge the tumor. Because it was on my spine, this could cause damage to my spinal cord and kill me. They felt that trying this method would be inhumane. At one point, we pleaded with them that I was going to die anyway, but these policies prevented us from being admitted to any of the trials that might have saved my life.

Only a year and a half earlier, I had been applying to various schools to continue my education. Now I was applying to clinical trials, just trying to continue breathing.

The problem is that, just like the Purdue campus, the most beautiful places are also the most well-traveled. In other words, the most promising options out there were ones that had already been tried; and for one reason or another, they would not work on me.

As I was throwing all this data at my brain, the chemotherapy began severely inhibiting my ability to process information. Everything in my brain began to slow down. It was like needing to run faster but finding your feet stuck in mud.

I also feared that all these declines could once again lead to more problems in my personal relationships, just as they did during my first bout. I didn't want this to happen again, so it required all my energy and focus to remain self-aware in this area. I tried hard to make sure I was thinking through things instead of just acting out of emotion. I knew God was still with me—that made all the difference.

Downward Turn

Toward the end of the spring semester, I no longer particularly enjoyed being on campus, which is really hard for me to admit even now. As you know, I loved being on campus. But the truth was, it was becoming more and more difficult for my mind to focus on anything other than the intense pain I was living with.

When I first got to college, my escape was being able to get out and do things, to be involved around campus. I camped in front of the football stadium, for heaven's sake! But when I couldn't get out anymore, it left me alone with my thoughts, which became harder and harder to live with. I found myself preferring to be home in Carmel more than being on campus, simply because my family was there supporting me. There were no expectations there other than just being and surviving another day.

I was taking a turn for the worse—and I knew it.

In May, I also noticed that my shoulder was becoming really sore. Having had multiple broken bones, I knew what one felt like—and this was *that* feeling. Sure enough, a PET scan revealed that there was a fracture on my clavicle caused by a new tumor.

My fourth tumor.

But it got worse. The same day, the scans also revealed that the tumor on my spine was not shrinking; it had more than doubled in size since we had started treating it with chemotherapy. Chemo wasn't working. They also found cancer spots in my lungs and in the lymph nodes located in my bronchi and throat area, which helped explain some of the problems I had been having with swallowing. The doctors told us what I was already beginning to assume: I was not going to make it. So I moved home and went into hospice care.

Leaving school broke my heart—because my heart was at Purdue.

The New, Unwanted Normal

As the tumor continued to grow, it greatly affected other parts of my body. I began losing function in my right leg, which made it hard for me to go up and down stairs. At first, I found a way to stretch out my leg and lift myself up by my arms, only letting the tips of my toes touch the steps, but we knew that this method couldn't work for long.

I was still fighting, but we were running out of ammo. I could tell that the whole process was really affecting my family—and there was nothing I could do about it except pray. My youngest brother, Ethan, was dealing with it all the best he could for his age—I really don't think it had hit him yet. Blake was having a harder time. He went down some paths that could really harm him, but family and friends—including our church community—continued to intervene and support our family. At times, I think we felt very alone, but the truth is, we had a lot more support than most people have in their lifetimes.

Blake eventually seemed to get to a better place. My dad also seemed to stop feeling the personal responsibility to quickly discover a cure for cancer. He stopped striving so hard and decided to focus on the time we had. It was hard, but his release of control over my situation seemed to help us all feel better.

And so we settled into a new, unwanted normal—one where my death was more likely than my survival. The chemo also robbed me of my hunger. I no longer wanted to eat—ever. So obviously, I lost a lot of weight. My critical thinking also continued to decline as well.

Again, I once heard that the three most painful things a human can endure are childbirth, passing kidney stones, and bone cancer. I could no longer hide the reality of how painful this had become. I hope that my words here help people understand how difficult and painful this process is—not so that more people will feel bad for me, but so they will be more diligent in raising funds, getting involved, and praying for and visiting those facing this and other cancers.

As I got sicker, more people came by the house to see me—by the hundreds. Friends. Sports figures. Family. Church community. In fact, one night, about three hundred people showed up in our yard to sing for me. They called it the Savior Serenade. News cameras were everywhere, and I was able to be propped up on the front porch to sing worship songs with those who loved me so much.

It was incredible, and it definitely brought me so much encouragement. I was not going to concede to cancer. Ever.

I knew my mobility was only going to continue to worsen, but I was still insistent on going back to campus in the fall semester of what was technically my sophomore year. Even though life at home was easier, I had made a commitment: I was going back to school. The best opportunities of my life were there—and I was not yet ready to abandon them.

I feared that my lack of mobility might limit these opportunities, specifically the chance to keep sharing my story and the hope of Christ with the nearly fifty thousand people on campus. I was hoping that God's answer to my prayer would continue.

Even as my brain struggled to keep up, this thought always remained in the back of my mind: I wanted to always be a good representation of Christ to everyone around me. This began with those precious ones who had surrounded me from the beginning—my family and friends—who had never left my side, no matter what. I wanted them to see the hope of Christ in me, even though they had seen the very worst in me.

I also wanted those who now knew my name to understand the hope I was still clinging to—a hope that I knew I would be fully experiencing in the life that would continue beyond this one. I didn't know how much time I had left, but I could only pray that I wasn't yet finished impacting those around and beyond me—providing hope and being a good steward of the opportunities that might come my way.

The best path to those opportunities still felt like they could be found at Purdue, so I decided that I was going back—no matter what.

Knocked Down, but Lifted Up

By the time the fall semester of 2018 rolled around, I was rolling myself around in a wheelchair. My parents were worried about my returning to school, but I don't think they had the heart to tell me I couldn't go.

We gave my roommates the heads-up—and really, an "out" if they wanted it. No pressure and no judgment. I was severely disabled at that point, something that would not only make my life very difficult, but also the lives of those living with me. Even so, my friends were champs; they said they really wanted to live with me anyway, and also that they wanted to help me in any way possible. What a huge reflection of God's work in all our lives. How many college sophomores do you know who would offer to help care for an almost completely disabled person between their own classes and events on campus?

A hospice team came to my dorm room four days a week to care for me. Beyond that, an incredible team of Purdue nursing students also came to help out one day each week. My roommates then handled the weekends. So with all this support, I moved back into the dorm, and we tried to make it work, but then *it* happened . . .

A seizure.

The seizure was a result of my tumor and the cancer now spreading to other parts of my body. I knew this wasn't good, but I kept it from my parents because I knew they would make me come home. Then one Sunday afternoon in September, while my mom and grandmother were visiting me on campus, I had another seizure in their presence. They had front-row seats to witness how severe it was; there was no hiding it from them.

After that, they really didn't have to convince me to come home. I knew it was time.

On September 29, 2018, the day that Purdue took down Nebraska, I tweeted the following: "Update: I'm sad to say I will not be making it back to #Purdue. My health has taken a turn for the worse, and the level of care I now need is too great. While I may not know how many days I have left, I'm trusting the one who does! #onlythestrong #boilerforlife #godsgotthis"

The next day, the senior captains and some of the coaching staff, led by my friend, David Blough, showed up at my house with the game ball from the Nebraska game. They gave me the ball, but then they gave me something I needed so much more: their prayers.

As the weeks passed, I worsened even more. I was going downhill fast. Around mid-October, my doctors told me I probably had about two, maybe two and a half months left to live. But oddly enough, more things related to living began to happen all around me. In other words, I was almost done here, but God wasn't yet done answering my prayer and revealing his hope through my story.

First of all, I began receiving phone calls and letters from people all over the world—from IU fans to Ohio State fans to the Purdue faithful. I received a phone call from Vice President Mike Pence, as well as Dabo Swinney, Tony Dungy, and many others. I can't even begin to remember all the other calls and visits I received from the Purdue and Colts organizations. They cared for me and my family with such selflessness. It was both humbling and overwhelming.

My family and friends were constantly there, spending time with me and loving me well. Friends like *Indianapolis Star* journalist Gregg Doyel, Colts General Manager Chris Ballard, and Trey Mock (the Colts mascot "Blue") were all regulars. Colts place-kicker Adam Vinatieri came by several times. Adrian Wojnarowski also made a special trip from the East Coast to visit—his kindness was overwhelming.

And of course, my close friend, David Blough, the quarterback of the Boilermakers, who had become like a spiritual brother to me, took every opportunity he could to encourage me. His quiet yet strong demeanor comforted me so many times as he showed me what it truly means to be a follower of Christ and a friend to his people.

Throughout my entire journey from the first diagnosis to this seemingly final prognosis, I was also constantly guided and loved well by my longtime youth pastor and friend, Joe Wittmer, as well as our pastor, Mark Vroegop, and my good friend, Scott McCoulgin. Joe had been with me throughout everything, writing scriptures for me on the doors of the hospital, playing board games with me for hours, and generally allowing me room to express weakness, doubt, anger, and pain with no judgment. His love toward me taught me so much about the steady love of Christ toward me. We would laugh together for hours on end. He will never know how much his patient strength brought joy to my life in the middle of what would have been impossible to bear alone.

Back when I was diagnosed for the second time, Scott felt divinely led to begin recording my thoughts on video. We sat eating salads at a McAllister's because I was basically on a keto diet due to the chemotherapy. His heart of purity was so evident, and I knew that God wanted to use my story, so I said yes. During much of this journey, Scott captured my thoughts on film.

Of course, we had no idea how much this would someday help in the writing process of the book you are now reading. Long before I knew what was ahead, God had already been at work in every part of my story.

I had to move downstairs from my bedroom because I could no longer navigate the stairs. We set up my hospice bed in the dining room of our house, which meant that I was the first person visitors would see when they walked through the front door—and they came by the droves every day.

In early October, a huge dream of mine became a reality: I became a college graduate. In light of the coursework I had completed and the time I had spent serving the community at Purdue, Dean Gary Bertoline graciously presented me an Associate of Science degree from Purdue Polytechnic Institute. This wasn't the way I had planned it, but God had seen me through to a finishing point in my short college career—and I was so very grateful.

You already know the next part—and this brings it all full circle, so to speak. God revealed that he wanted to do even more with my story when ESPN's Tom Rinaldi stopped by the house and recorded interviews with my family and me. After the complication with my kidneys caused my near-death experience that week, followed by our incredible upset win over Ohio State, life somehow seemed to speed up instead of slow down, even as my ability to live was slowing by the week.

Even so, another one of my big life dreams came true in late October. I had always wanted to be an analyst on SportsCenter—and on the 24th, I joined Scott Van Pelt for a ten-minute interview on the show. His kindness and concern affected me in deeply meaningful ways, but what I loved the most about him was that he also let me just talk sports.

Who could have ever imagined such a crazy turn of events? It all felt so incredibly surreal—experiencing so much life while also experiencing the sensation of dying.

CHAPTER 20

Endings and Beginnings

(Tyler)

The moment had finally arrived when I was certain that I would die. It felt that it was only a matter of time. Death is something that most people don't want to think about, but to me, it has become a familiar subject of thought and conversation.

Only four years earlier, I had decided that either my tumor would kill me or I would. The idea of waiting for death with no hope was so horrific to me that I was ready to take control of my situation and hurry it along. But God had truly transformed my perspective since my first cancer bout.

Whispers and Shouts

My viewpoint of death has changed. It is now something to look forward to because I know I'll be in heaven with my savior. I am looking forward to being pain-free for the first time in almost five years. When it comes to the topic of death, I now have hope.

Where does my hope come from?

C. S. Lewis once said, "God whispers to us in our pleasures, speaks in our conscience, but shouts in our pains: it is his megaphone to rouse a deaf world."[1] This has become so true in my life—God has gotten through to me using the vehicle of my pain. Not in a cruel way, but in a kind way, using the fallenness of my nature and this world to reveal to me a peace that is bigger and higher than this life on Earth.

Someone once asked me what exactly God is shouting in people's pain. Honestly, I think God shouts a lot of things, and I don't think I should be one to put words in his mouth. But if I had to interpret what he has been shouting to me in the course of my life and story, it would be this: it might be hard right now in the moment, but it's all going to pay off someday in another place. I might not be able to see and fully comprehend my purpose and the impact I've had in this life, but one day I will.

My pastors began talking to me about what I want my funeral to be like. I told them that I hope people will be able to clearly see Christ and the work he has done, not just in my life, but also in the lives of all the other people I've met and affected who will carry this same hope for themselves and for others. I also hope people will see the need for donating to pediatric cancer research so that other kids don't have to go through the same things I've been through.

I don't want even a single other child to have to spend five years of his or her life fighting to pursue dreams. I hope my fight will make a difference in other children's fights. And as I reflect on the incredible fact that Christ has allowed me to live this long, my prayer is that the extra time he has graciously afforded me to stay here will create more time for someone else.

People used to call me Smiley, so I really hope that when people leave my funeral, they leave a smile. But above all, I hope that my funeral will reflect my constant, underlying thought over the past few years: that my continuing story and the platform given to me through it are nothing but chances to bring glory to God.

Glory just means light. My hope has been that the shadows and darkness of the backdrop of my story will make the light more evident and easier to see . . . a light that reveals the hope available to all of us through a grace stronger than the sufferings and doubts of this life.

---

1   C. S. Lewis, *The Problem of Pain* (London: The Centenary Press, 1940), n.p.

Jesus has provided me with a very certain peace, which has helped me have somewhat of a clear mind to be able to share my story in a terrible situation. Without God providing me with emotional support, it would be very, very difficult for me to stand in front of a room of people—or even in front of my family and friends—and share about the things I'm going through without breaking down into fits of rage and crying . . . because that's how difficult this life sometimes is. It's not that being angry or crying are bad things; I just mean that they would make it really hard for me to get through the process of doing interviews or talking to groups of people. But Christ has definitely provided me with supernatural strength and emotional peace to be able to speak out. And even when I'm alone, this peace is still with me, reminding me that whatever happens is going to be used for my good and for the good of others.

He has shown me an incredible light in the middle of this incredible darkness.

Please don't think I'm crazy here. Yes, I had other ideas about the ways I wanted this story to end. But I can now say with confidence that I'm really okay with whatever God has planned for me. I trust that his plan is bigger and better than mine. Even if I don't understand the plan, I trust the heart of the planner.

God has continually reminded me which part of his plan I *can* actually know and understand. It all comes back to the scripture he brought to me around the time of my first diagnosis: "Rejoice always, pray continually, give thanks in all circumstances; for this is God's will for you in Christ Jesus" (1 Thessalonians 5:16–18, NIV). This clear direction has given me such freedom. When I feel lost and have no idea what to do, I know I can still rejoice, pray, and give thanks, no matter the circumstance. What a gift this clarity has brought me! It is an anchor.

He didn't say to give thanks only in the *good* circumstances, but in *all* circumstances. C. S. Lewis was right; I've found that God has used my pain as a megaphone to reveal to me that God is kind, trustworthy, and in the process of redeeming all the brokenness, cancer, and pain in this world. Someday he will finish this work of redemption, but for now, I have to wait. Even so, God's grace has proven to be more than enough for me. And just as Christ did for us, I can use my pain to bring healing and comfort to others who feel like they are alone.

But why is God waiting so long to finish his big story?

That's a fair question. It is easy to feel that he must not care about our suffering, or else he would not leave us to face it for even another minute. It hurts—and I know this pain well. But just because *it* hurts does not mean *he* is trying to hurt us. He is actually trying to save and heal us, along with as many people who will let him heal them as well.

The message of Jesus is not just as simple as we have "bad" sin and he has "good" forgiveness. It actually comes to life within a context much more radical and relational: that God himself chose to become a man so he could know what it feels like to be us. He didn't stay far away but instead chose to come and suffer with us, which is why one of his names (Immanuel) means "God with us." He experienced every bit of the pain we experience, but in higher doses. He didn't have to do this, but he chose to so he can empathize with our sufferings and weaknesses, having known them for himself (see Hebrews 4:15).

Again, it's the in-between—the middle part—that we struggle with . . . this difficult time of waiting for him to redeem all things and end all this suffering. But even his waiting is an expression of his grace; he wants everyone to have a chance to respond to the great love he has poured out on the whole world. "But do not overlook this one fact, beloved, that with the Lord one day is as a thousand years, and a thousand years as one day. The Lord is not slow to fulfill his promise as some count slowness, but is patient toward you, not wishing that any should perish, but that all should reach repentance " (2 Peter 3:8–9, ESV).

He may be waiting to finish the story, but he has not left us alone or without hope . . . and I know that heaven will be worth the wait. When my funeral is over, whenever that is, I hope that people leave with both tears and smiles, mourning my loss, but also remembering why this is actually a happy occasion. It may be hard in the moment for those here on Earth, but if they hear the hope I have heard in this short life, then we can all be together in heaven. I also hope that my friends and my precious family know how much I love them and how deeply thankful I am for everything they have taught me through their words, their actions, and in their amazingly selfless care for me during these past five years.

I'm continually reminded of what Paul said about gains and losses: "But whatever were gains to me I now consider loss for the sake of Christ. What is more, I consider everything a loss because of the surpassing worth of knowing Christ Jesus my Lord, for whose sake I have lost all things. I consider them garbage, that I may gain Christ and be found in him . . . " (Philippians 3:7–9, NIV).

All that I could have gained in this life I now see as loss. So much of it has been great, but from a comparison standpoint, it is like garbage compared to what God has for me just around the corner. He has proven his goodness to me so many times, and I know he will prove it to me even more when I cross into the next part of the eternal life he has created for me. But even here, he has given me incredible blessings, like being able to work with ESPN, a lifelong dream of mine, or to go on *Good Morning America* and countless other media outlets to talk about my passion for cancer research and the hope I have in Christ.

At every turn, God has opened doors—obvious doors. As a person who has felt completely confused when it comes to my health, these clearly marked doors have been incredible encouragements. And even when I haven't known what to do next, I have learned to rejoice, pray, give thanks, and just walk forward through the next door God is opening—doors that have led me to places beyond my wildest dreams.

And another door, the one that God will open when I pass away, will lead me to an even better dream.

The ultimate story . . . the ultimate message that I pray comes through these pages and reflections is this: there is hope. There always has been and always will be. No matter the choices you have made in your life, there is always hope. There is always an opportunity to leave a legacy. There is always an opportunity to help heal others' hurts.

All we can do is live out the stories we have. When I was diagnosed for the second time, a light came on inside me. I saw the hope that is found in Christ and the opportunity I had to live out my unique story in the days to come. I saw that Christ wanted to do special things in my life and in the lives of others. I didn't know to what extent, but I knew that he wanted to make my life count for more than just living or dying. There were no words to fully explain it. I just knew.

It is my prayer that through this story and these words, you will also catch a glimpse of the God who has sustained me through the unthinkable and " . . . perhaps feel [your] way toward him and find him. Yet he is actually not far from each one of us . . . " (Acts 17:27, ESV).

I was once far away from Christ, too, but he was never far away from me. And Christ is never far away from you, either. His love is the ultimate upset that overcomes all the other reasons in life that we have to be upset.

Take it from a terminal underdog who has lived—and I mean, really lived—to tell about it.

CHAPTER 21

Finishing Big . . . Finishing Well

There are many other excerpts and interviews that captured Tyler's thoughts and sentiments throughout the course of his life. But as he drew nearer to the end, it was this moment in the real-time story when his condition severely limited his ability to think and speak clearly.

Much was compiled and edited after that moment in time and after his death. This chapter chronicles some of the major events that occurred during his final days.

Atlanta

Tyler was obviously at the brink of death, but even this didn't stop him from still pursuing every opportunity that came his way. On November 28, he was invited to a fundraising luncheon for cancer research at Riley—an event called Be the Hope Now. At the end of the event, he was called up to the stage. Indiana Governor Eric Holcomb appeared on a screen and presented Tyler with the Sagamore of the Wabash, the highest civilian honor in the state of Indiana. Tyler was humbled and moved by this honor, realizing again that God was not yet done with his life and story.

This realization continued when Tyler and his family received the stunning news in early December that he was being awarded the Disney Spirit Award, the highest honor presented to college football's most inspirational player, coach, team, or figure. The Trents boarded a private jet generously provided by ESPN for the trip to Atlanta and to the College Football Hall of Fame, where the award would be presented on December 6. By that point, Tyler was severely disabled and struggling mentally, but he would not be denied this next open door of opportunity to share the hope he so deeply believed in.

The event in Atlanta was a barrage of activity, definitely producing many challenges to a young man nearing the end. Being rolled around in a wheelchair, Tyler still insisted on attending every luncheon, interview, and event on the docket leading up to the College Football Awards Show, which was slated to be broadcast live to the entire nation.

As the elite of the elite among collegiate football's players and personalities came and went through the convention center, Tyler stole the show as fans lined the red carpet to take his picture. He did interviews with multiple ESPN personalities, sometimes being barely able to speak only a few hours or minutes before. It was as if he had all the strength he needed exactly when he needed it.

But behind the scenes, he was really struggling. He was exhausted and often very emotional due to the hospice medication that was trying to keep his incredible pain at bay. Tony and Kelly had to call his hospice team in Indianapolis and request that additional medication and supplies be drop-shipped to the hotel as soon as possible. These kinds of logistical challenges were just a part of their reality.

Ethan and Blake were in tow, shopping in the gift shops, asking their parents for extra spending money, and eating in food courts, as if they were just another family on another trip. In this way, the Trent family soaked up every moment they could with Tyler by just trying to have as many normal experiences together as possible, even though everything happening to them was far from normal. Blake, an inquisitive and technologically capable young man, captured much of the experience on his phone that was mounted to one of the latest handheld steady-cam devices. He often interviewed Tyler between events, asking probing questions about his outlook on the whole experience. Ethan was right there with them, asking questions and pushing his brother's wheelchair.

They were accompanied on the trip by Matt Rector, the Associate Strategic Communications Director for Purdue Football, and David Blough. Matt and David never left the family's side, spending time talking with each of the Trents and often pushing Tyler's wheelchair through the hotel and convention center. Everywhere they went, fans and players stopped to meet Tyler and get pictures with him and his entourage.

Once the nationally televised program began and ESPN *College GameDay* anchor Chris Fowler began doling out awards to outstanding players from across the nation, a palpable anticipation began to build for Tyler's upcoming presentation because it was being constantly foreshadowed in previews before each commercial break. During one of those breaks, Dabo Swinney, the head football coach at Clemson University, left his chair near the front row and made his way to introduce himself to Tyler in person; they had only spoken on the phone. Countless other coaches, players, and media personalities also sought Tyler out to offer him their support and encouragement.

When the moment finally came, David Blough rolled Tyler into the spotlight on an international stage. He was met with a very long standing ovation. Tom Rinaldi then began the interview with his characteristic tone of gentleness and compassion, pointing out to Tyler that the "luminaries" of the sport of college football had just stood to applaud him for more than a minute.

"In my mind, I don't deserve it," Tyler muttered weakly.

Rinaldi responded by asking Tyler why he repeatedly insisted that he didn't deserve all that had come his way.

"Because a year ago," Tyler replied, "I prayed that I would have the opportunity to share my story—and now it's coming true."

In his weakened state, he had not answered Rinaldi's question directly, but his point was still clear. Tyler felt undeserving of all the attention and praise because he knew that the origin of both was not his own life or story. Rather, Tyler felt that this once-in-a-lifetime moment was the result of someone else's miraculous involvement. Tyler wanted the attention pointed toward the divine intervention that had brought him to this unlikely moment in an equally unlikely spotlight. Rinaldi then asked him what his message was to the millions of people who had been touched by his story.

"At the end of the day, there is always a light at the end of the tunnel. As long as you rely on your faith, things will work out." He looked Rinaldi in the eyes and shook his head affirmatively as he spoke these words that he had come to believe with all his heart.

Rinaldi then turned the attention to the young man now sitting to his left, David Blough. He asked him why he wanted to come to Atlanta to be with Tyler and his family during this moment.

"Well, Tyler exemplifies everything about the Purdue community," the Boilermakers quarterback said. "He's united us all. We love him, and we're incredibly proud of him and what he means, like you said, to millions and millions of people. So Tyler is an inspiration to so many, and it's just an honor to get to be a part of his story and to get to share his faith and his testimony."

Rinaldi then turned his attention to Tyler's shoes, which once belonged to Craig Segar, the beloved broadcaster who passed away from cancer in 2016. Segar's wife, Stacy, gave the shoes to Tyler as a gift. Then Rinaldi called for everyone present who considered themselves to be on Tyler's team to stand and show him their support—and another very long standing ovation ensued.

After the presentation, Tyler and his family were whisked away by event personnel to speak to the media. They boarded an elevator for the second floor of the venue, which is where a separate media room and reception area overlooked the main event space through tall, soundproof panes of glass. Tyler was rolled off the elevator only a few feet from the Heisman Trophy, the College Football Playoff National Championship Trophy, and a slew of other trophies and awards protected under glass.

But when Tyler came off the elevator, his attention immediately went not to those icons of achievement in athletics that he had worked so long as a writer and journalist to be near; rather, he turned his attention to his father, Tony. Tony leaned down, and the two shared a long, tearful embrace, speaking softly to each other after Tyler's big moment.

It was a happy moment, but there was also a palpable sadness in the air. Even the members of the media, most of whom had never met Tyler, seemed to feel it. Everyone sensed that Tyler had met his final goal—to accept this award and share his faith with the world one last time. The moment was so huge, but so was the emotional letdown in its aftermath.

No one wanted Tyler's incredible ride to come to an end . . . we were all on the ride with him.

After a barrage of camera flashes, poses, and questions, Tyler was exhausted. His youngest brother, Ethan, took note of his condition and began piling up a plate of nachos and queso dip, seemingly doing so for himself, as any young teenager might do. Then he walked up with the plate and asked his big brother, "Hey Tyler, are you hungry?"

The media and event hosts recognized what was happening and gave the Trents a little room to breathe as Tyler sat with both of his brothers at a small table overlooking the event that was still going on in the room beneath them. Both younger brothers were attentive to the needs of their older sibling in that moment.

Blake took out his camera and began asking Tyler questions about everything that had just occurred. His deep questions and compelling insight were far beyond those of a normal eighteen-year-old. In that moment, not knowing how many more they would have together, they immersed themselves in a familiar place—the kind of conversation known only by brothers. Honest. Raw. Sometimes full of banter. But real—a supremely sweet reflection of the love they had for one another, but also the sadness of what now lay ahead of them.

But the night wasn't quite over. A phone call came in from the producers of the show *NBA on TNT*, hosted by Ernie Johnson, Shaquille O'Neil, Kenny Smith, and Charles Barkley. Because the show is also recorded in Atlanta, they asked if Tyler and the family would be willing to join them in their studio for an interview later that night. Tyler was exhausted, but he would not miss even a single drop of the experience God was pouring over him.

A van ride across town found the Trents and David sharing an evening with these NBA legends. Their conversations were deep and impactful, reaching far beyond sports and into what really matters in life: suffering, community, and the faith under which Tyler and his family were taking shelter. Even though Tyler had trouble at times during the trip being mentally present, it seemed that every time a new opportunity to talk presented itself, he was suddenly able again.

The evening and event finally ended, and Tyler and his family were spent. The plane ride back to Indianapolis the next day was filled with bittersweet reflections. Tyler's back pain was accelerating, as was his mental fogginess from the growing tumors and the hospice medications regulating his pain. It was back to his bed at his house in Carmel. His ride on the roller coaster God had prepared for him as an answer to his prayer about letting his story shine light on the grace and hope of Christ had seemingly come to a halt.

But God had one more experience up his sleeve . . . one last exhilarating turn for Tyler.

Nashville

The Purdue football team had won enough games to become bowl eligible, just like Tyler had predicted. They were invited to Nashville to face a formidable SEC opponent, the Auburn Tigers, in the Music City Bowl, which was being hosted at Nissan Stadium, home of the Tennessee Titans. Representatives of the Music City Bowl reached out to the Trents and offered them a gracious invitation to attend as their guests of honor—and for Tyler to serve as the Honorary Captain for both teams at the center of the field for the opening coin toss.

The incredible outpouring of love toward Tyler kept coming when Jim Irsay, owner of the Indianapolis Colts, also offered the Trents use of the Colts' private jet to make the trip to Nashville. Tyler was fading, but the Music City Bowl offered him yet another chance to keep living life to the fullest all the way up to his final moment, which everyone knew could come at any time.

The trip to Nashville was the most difficult of all for Tyler and his family. They were cordially offered plush accommodations at the world-famous Gaylord Opryland Resort. Kelly and Tony had their hands full trying to help Tyler make it through all the demands of being at the event. Media meetings. Luncheons. Dinners. Interviews. Tyler wanted to do them all, and he did everything asked of him. It was as if he was running on spiritual fumes. Between these commitments, Tyler would lie in a hospital bed that had been brought into their hotel room, falling in and out of consciousness as he tried to rest and gain just a little more strength.

The Trents were accompanied by many friends and family on the trip to Nashville, including Cathy Campbell, Kelly's mom and Tyler's beloved grandmother, who visited him daily with a Starbucks cup and a smile; Tony's sister, Trisha Shuman, and her husband and children, Jeff, Hallee, and Trent; and Tony's parents, Martin and Glenna Trent. They were also joined by Scott McCouglin, Tyler's friend and videographer, and Trey Mock, the mascot for the Indianapolis Colts, who had become a dear friend to Tyler during his struggle.

Everyone chipped in to help as much as they could, even when that meant clearing the room so Tyler could try to sleep. Sleep was elusive to him at that point. He had learned to sleep with headphones to block out any distractions that might break his delicate restfulness, but even these didn't seem to be helping anymore.

On the morning of December 28, the day of the Music City Bowl, Tyler expressed to his parents that he wasn't sure he could go. His pain and fatigue were beginning to get the best of him. The family said a prayer together, and Kelly told him it would be just fine if he stayed and rested. It was all meant to be something for him to enjoy, not for him to suffer through. She told him that everyone would understand, and surely they would have.

But it was as if their prayer and talk somehow energized Tyler like a recharged, albeit weak battery. He was the Honorary Captain of the game, and he would not let his friends and comrades down. He shared a few inspirational words[2] and then insisted on going to the game because he didn't want to let his Purdue team down.

They made their way to Nissan Stadium, and Tyler was rolled out onto the field to the cheers of thousands of people. He did his part and "stood" proudly by his Boilermaker co-captains with honor, loyalty, and courage.

After the coin toss, the family made its way back to the tunnel to head to the suite where they would watch the game. Before they could even get through the tunnel, Tyler began taking a sharp turn for the worst. His pain became unbearable, so much so that by the time they made it to the suite, he was in and out of consciousness for

---

2   See the epilogue for Trey Mock's memory about Tyler's comments at this moment.

most of the game.

The Boilermakers took a beating that day—as did Tyler. Throughout the fall of 2018, it had seemed as if Tyler's health and the football team's performance had mysteriously mirrored each other. Regardless, they supported each other through thick and thin. Their upset of Ohio State was also a huge personal upset for Tyler—a day many didn't think he'd survive to see but that was used to magnify Tyler's story and his hope around the world. Purdue's bowl bid was a final chance to either win or go down fighting, just as it was for Tyler, who began going down for the last time, fighting until the very end.

It seemed that when Purdue's season ended, Tyler's season ended as well. Football was just the backdrop. Brotherhood, hope, endurance, and abiding love are the real story—and these were intimately shared between the young men on the field and a particular young man in a wheelchair.

The trip back to Indianapolis was wrought with difficulty. Tyler's season was over, and everyone knew it. Four days later, on New Year's Day, Tyler experienced the ultimate upset when the eternal life he had already been granted through a relationship with Jesus Christ changed locations from this earth to the location his savior had prepared for him. When he died, he was surrounded by his friends and family, who served and loved him well to the very end.

He was never alone, and his hope was never vanquished . . . as his last written words reveal.[3]

---

3   The final two articles written by Tyler are in chapter 23.

CHAPTER 22

It's a Devastating, Wonderful Life

(Tony & Kelly)

This book is not over. Tyler will have the last word. After all, it's his book.

But before he shares his final thoughts, we feel compelled to reveal just a bit more about the crippling loss that parents, friends, and families experience during and after cancer. Tyler's dream was to raise awareness and funds for the research so that fewer people will ever have to experience what we've been through. So we want to honor his dream by offering an honest and candid glimpse into some of the darker parts of this journey.

This chapter has been by far the most difficult to complete. We are devastated and grieving as we write it. And while there are so many positives to celebrate and focus on, in this moment, we feel that you need to really see the whole picture so you can understand how to empathize with those who are living right now in the situation we have lived in for five years. To be clear, though we will speak from a painfully honest place, we have not lost our hope. We have not lost our faith.

But we have lost our son . . . for now.

The Devastation of Loss

The pain is staggering, even as we feel the gracious comfort that our family, our faith, and our community are so diligently providing. Without their presence and our hope, our loss would be so unbearable that it would destroy us. The anchors that kept Tyler tethered down when pain and despair attempted to whisk him away into the darkness are also keeping us from blowing away. The only confidence we have is in these anchors for the soul—nothing else remains for us. The pain of what we've lost is difficult to explain. It is connected to a million other things that *once were* or that *will never be* because our son's life here is no more.

The loss of all that once was important to Tyler is simply heartbreaking. As you know, he lost so much of his identity as a leader and as a friend during his first bout. Cancer robbed him of time and opportunities. It robbed him of fun. It robbed him of trips and experiences and laughter and the normal kind of angst that every teenager feels. His angst was heavier than most. He really never got to be a "normal" teenager.

We know that "normal" is a relative thing; it really doesn't exist. We know that there are millions in this world who don't have a "normal" American existence and would be so grateful for even a single day in the life that Tyler had before the cancer came. We are not trying to complain from a privileged, first-world viewpoint. We get it. Tyler was loved, had everything he needed, and still had more opportunities in this life as a child and young adult than nine of out ten people in this world will have if they live a hundred years.

It's easy to do that—to inadvertently or even intentionally add a context of guilt and entitlement to the normal, healthy process of grieving. It can even seem logical and justifiable, but grief is not a logical path. It is an emotional and spiritual one. Our pastor, Mark Vroegop, talks a lot about the biblical act of *lamenting*, something that we, in the modern age, often overlook. We try to stay positive and avert our eyes from what is uncomfortable and can't be easily explained, hoping that if we don't acknowledge that something that is ripping us apart, it will eventually just go away on its own someday.

And so we bury our pain, not realizing that by doing so, we're not actually burying it; we're planting it. And what grows from unresolved, not-fully-felt seeds of mourning and anguish is a life of future bitterness, depression, anxiety, and anger that seems to "come out of nowhere" when we least expect it. Most things don't come out of nowhere . . . they come out of somewhere, a place deep inside we've never allowed ourselves to fully feel or address. We can't bear to respond as Job from the Bible responded to his own devastating losses—by sitting in the ashes and crying out in pain.

As Tyler's parents, we don't want to avoid this moment to lament, to cry out in pain. We don't want to rationalize our loss with the slant of a modern American perspective that answers every expression of loss with "at least": *At least Tyler knew that you loved him. At least he got to live on this earth for twenty years; some kids don't even get that long. At least his life made a difference.*

These things may all be true, but rarely is an "at least" the best approach to deal with a devastating loss. When we deal with grieving people this way, we inadvertently dismiss the real, present legitimacy of what they are feeling, trying to bypass it so that we don't have to feel it with them. It is a way to circumvent the discomfort of empathy—to try to contrive some silly silver lining instead of just sitting next to someone under their black cloud. The bottom line is, we are afraid we won't be able to endure the rain and cold they are having to endure, so we find a way to observe and advise from a distance instead of sitting and hurting *with* them.

The "at leasts" of our story may be true, but they are of little comfort right now. They may come into the picture later, when we have gone through a long, difficult process of grieving, but they are just not where we are today. Today, we are going to sit in these ashes and cry . . . and there is no "at least" that should keep us from doing so.

Tyler didn't just lose relationships; he also lost opportunities. For me (Tony), the loss of experiences in college and his paid internship at BP Oil in Chicago are realities that hit me especially hard. I think he just wanted to experience life as an adult—that transition from being a boy to becoming a man who learns to work hard, earn a living, and figure out what it means to take the next steps in life. Because of his sickness, he had to stop taking those steps, even when they were offered to him. It breaks my heart in a deep way, probably because every father wants to help his son take those steps into manhood. I'll never get to do that with my oldest son.

We feel the pain over the loss of his mobility in the last few years. Tyler had to learn the hard way what it means to live as a disabled individual on a college campus. The Purdue administration and his disability advisor were amazing from the get-go. From day one, before anyone knew who he was, he was already important to them. They changed classrooms for him. They gave him a parking pass so he could park anywhere on campus, even in spots reserved for university staff. They went above and beyond to make it work for him—and we are so grateful. In fact, this experience produced in Tyler a sense of compassion for the disabled community. He empathized with them on a deep level.

But we mourn the fact that this was so difficult for him—the process of exposing his pain to everyone. During his first year on campus, he rarely told anyone he had cancer. He didn't want anyone to look at him differently or think that he was expecting preferential treatment. But he was bald and walking on crutches in the beginning—and was in a wheelchair at the end. He couldn't hide his disability, and it caused him a lot of inconvenience and suffering.

We feel the loss of his academic potential. He was a brilliant kid who went to Purdue on the Presidential Scholarship. Who knows how much he might have accomplished from a scholastic perspective if he had just had more time—and if he had been afforded all the faculties that his incredibly sharp mind once possessed. Though we know that God will ensure nothing is wasted in the end, it certainly feels like a waste right now.

We mourn the loss of Tyler's on-campus role as a sports writer and fan. When he camped out—something we questioned at the time, asking him if he really thought it best to go straight from chemotherapy to sleeping outside on the concrete—he lit a fire under the Purdue students and the fan base. He helped build momentum for Purdue athletics, painting his face and body and wildly cheering like a lunatic in the student section. He loved every minute of it. He became the life of the Purdue party, and they loved him deeply. And though we have fond memories of those times, those times are now gone. It hurts.

Looking back, the memories of having to break unbearable news to our son still wounds our hearts today. Having to tell him not once, not twice, but three times that he had cancer is something we pray no parent ever has to do . . . but we know someone will have to do it. We had to do it, and this is one of the reasons why this book has been written.

When Tyler had just returned from having the time of his life covering the Big Ten Basketball Tournament at Madison Square Garden in New York, we took him to dinner. He thought we were just going out to catch up, so he went on and on about the incredible experience. He was so alive and excited to finally be living the early stages of the life he had always dreamed of. It felt like we were hiding a knife, just waiting to stab him with the news that his cancer had spread to his spine. It felt cruel, but we had to tell him.

What I (Tony) wanted to tell my son was that he didn't have to do this anymore. I wanted to tell him that life didn't have to be so hard for him anymore. I wanted to tell him that he was going to be able to live like a normal teenager. Instead, I added to his devastation. I was always the bearer of the worst news. He wept when we told him. He kept asking, "Why? Why?" I had no answer. We drove home in tears as he went back in his dorm. His friends met him there and tried to comfort him, but the truth was, none of us could remove his pain.

After the May MRI revealed the fourth tumor on his clavicle and the fact that the tumor on his spine had grown significantly, we officially pulled him out of school, and he entered hospice care back at home. They thought he had between two weeks and two months to live. At first, we thought he would be gone soon, but he kept having moments of comeback—each one feeling like an upset. Each one giving us more time with our boy . . . more time for him to accomplish God's purposes in his life.

He remained in hospice care during the whole summer. By July, after reading *When Breath Becomes Air*, he had decided to go back to school, even though he knew his time here was very limited. Obviously, we were very worried. We told him that he would have to prove to us he could get in and out of bed, get himself to the bathroom, and the like. These skills would be necessary if he was going to move an hour away and live on campus again. He worked so hard to meet these goals, to make a plan so it would work. And he tried it, but after the seizures began, once again, he had to abandon the plan he had worked so hard to put into motion. When we brought him home after witnessing his seizure, he told us he had not urinated in four days. His body was in a toxic state. That was when his doctors surgically implanted nestrophomy tubes to help his kidneys to begin functioning again.

I (Tony) also mourn the time that I turned into a desperate father and made life hard on Tyler and the whole family. I am kind of a control freak anyway, but when the doctors couldn't find another step to take, I took matters into my own hands. I became a medical tyrant, traveling the country and calling anyone around the world who might be able to help.

In fact, Tyler began calling me "Daddy Doctor" during this time, changing my contact in his phone to this new title. He even bought me a medical book as a gift, poking at me in fun, but also showing me love in my desperation. Every time I heard another "no" for my son—a "no" from someone who had the medicine in in-hand that might be able to save him—I was furious on a level I can't really explain. The location of the tumor—near his spine—kept anyone from being able to keep trying new and radical methods because of the fear of killing Tyler in the process.

Tyler was the one dying, but each door that closed in our faces killed us, too—one rejection at a time.

What Might Have Been

It is not just what we experienced that breaks our hearts, but also what we will now never get to experience. We have not just lost a son; we have also lost the dreams for what his life might have been. We have lost the daughter-in-law whom he will never get to marry. We have lost the grandchildren who would have been born to our firstborn.

I (Tony) recently attended a wedding, and I had to leave. It was just too painful knowing that my boy will never see his bride walking down the aisle toward him, dressed in white. He will never have a wedding night or a honeymoon. He will never know what it means to have brothers-in-law and sisters-in-law. We will never get to have the uncomfortable conversations with him and his wife about how they should divide their time at the holidays between our family and his in-laws. His kids will never run through our house in pajamas on their way to open up way too many presents from way-too-proud grandparents.

When we returned from Atlanta and the whole experience at the College Football Hall of Fame and the Disney Spirit Award, Tyler began expressing the fact that he might never experience getting married and having kids. We know that God will restore all things in time, but for now, we're literally at a loss.

I (Kelly) could tell that Tyler was really struggling with seeing his friends reach milestones that he knew he would never cross. It was bittersweet for him, especially with his three or four lifelong friends. He loved them the most, so it hurt him the most. He had been through life with them from birth to college—but he was facing death alone, not in the sense of not having them around to support him, but in the heavy reality that he would enter death without them, and they would enter the next parts of their lives without him.

This is hard on us as well. It is a reality we have to live with and grow in. Our best family friends celebrate graduations, weddings, new jobs, and everything else that all parents hope for their children. We are happy for these milestones in their children's lives, but we are constantly aware of the crushing sense of loss we feel because Tyler will never experience these joyous moments. Again, there is no "at least" that can make this pain go away. We have two other boys with whom we will hopefully get to experience these things, and for that we are grateful. They are equally as important to us as Tyler, but they cannot and should not be expected to replace Tyler. "At least you have two other sons who will grow up" is not something that makes this loss go away.

Let me (Kelly) be very clear here. I am so excited for my friends and family members with children—thrilled to hear all that is going on in their lives. The feeling of bittersweetness is something I wish I didn't feel, because I want—and choose—to celebrate with them. It is obviously not their fault that my son died of cancer at a young age. On the contrary, they have been God-sent friends and family who have been present at every winding turn, and they are deeply heartbroken along with us.

We lost Tyler, but they lost him, too. His friends and his cousins are the very people with whom he did everything in life. They have cancelled trips and moved their lives around, not wanting to be away if and when Tyler were to take a turn for the worst. These people are precious to me, and their kids are like my own, just as my kids are like their own.

But it's still extremely hard—a reality of what it means to suffer this kind of loss. Even before Tyler died, it was a struggle—one we felt guilty to be having—to see other families have "normal" experiences. It comes out in hidden anger or jealousy, usually not voiced out loud, but still there. When you see someone's pictures on social media of a camping trip or a vacation, it's hard not to think, *That will never happen with my family again.*

That being said, we are so incredibly grateful for the beautiful experiences that God, through generous people, afforded us during Tyler's long struggle. We experienced things that very few people ever will, and those memories do help a lot. Going to bowl games, Pacers games, Colts games, home games, away games, Hawaii, Atlanta, and Nashville—these moments affected us deeply. They are irreplaceable memories that helped not only Tyler but also our whole family. Our other two boys were noticeably happier during these experiences because they gave us temporary moments of relief—time to breathe and not focus completely on the tragedy of what was happening. For these, our hearts remain eternally appreciative. But there were also a lot of things we contemplated doing during those days that we knew could never happen because Tyler's condition would prevent them from being possible—that is just the realistic bitter side of the sweetness.

I (Kelly) have been blessed to be able to have some of these raw conversations about my struggles with my closest girlfriends, with whom I live in close, faith-based community. It could come off as ungrateful and offensive to express what I'm feeling, but they have never made me feel that way. And they get to tell me the honest way they are feeling, too. Having a safe place to be honest—even ugly honest—has been such a beautiful thing that I know I will continue to need for the rest of my life. The truth is, everyone needs it. I hope to be able to be there for them as they walk out their own challenges with their families, as they have done with me.

The reality of living in a state of mourning is a strange combination of grief and gratitude. Both are so important, and neither should be overlooked. Feeling what we are feeling is so hard, but it would be worse to try to not feel it—to push it down and bury it. It's hard not to do this, but we are trying, and we need people to help us continue down the path of honesty and recovery.

What the Cameras Couldn't Show

I (Tony) wish this wasn't the case, but it is a dagger to me when I hear people complain about what seems to me to be very small problems. I know that this is not really fair since people can't fully know about something that they've never experienced, but it is still my knee-jerk, emotional reaction. I'm working on it. But the bottom line is that people really don't know, and this is something we can help remedy through this book.

Friends have told us that they didn't understand what we had to go through until they watched the ESPN piece and saw us picking up a painfully groaning Tyler out of his bed to transfer him to his wheelchair. This let us know that it is hard for others to understand the reality of what it means to care for someone with cancer or someone who is disabled. Again, we don't want to bring attention to ourselves, but rather to help people understand what real life has been like for our son and for us so that they will be more motivated and mobilized to join the fight to end cancer.

The cameras couldn't show the deep sadness we felt in helping our son do the simplest of tasks that he had once been so very capable of doing on his own. Tyler was always in motion, helping other people, picking them up or dropping them off in his car when they needed a ride. He was always the first one to jump in when someone needed a hand, constantly helping with events at school or church. He had worked a job since he was thirteen years old. To then see this once extremely self-sufficient young man crying his eyes out because he could not help his own mother carry something in from the car—this wrecked us in ways we can't describe.

There were endless complications and horrible situations that we constantly endured in caring for him. Before he had to finally come back home that last semester, he took a fall in his dorm room and couldn't get back up. He had to call his roommates to come help. He had several falls at our house as well. Once he fell coming in from our garage and had to just lie there until he could reach me (Kelly) on the phone. I was next door at the neighbor's house and ran immediately to help him up. The next day, he fell in the bathroom upstairs, which is when we decided to move his bedroom downstairs into the dining room because he had become such a fall risk.

It was so difficult to watch him try so hard but not be able to accomplish easy tasks. When he had lost so much function in his right leg, I (Tony) would work with him for hours as he tried to just position it or lift it enough to create some kind of new process that would let him maintain a level of mobility. In pain and frustration, he would just keep trying. I was so proud of him, watching him "huff and puff" up what seemed to him to be mountains—like the little engine that could. *I think I can. I think I can. I think I can.*

But eventually, he just couldn't.

Once he was nearing complete disability, our daily life was not a pretty process. Again, our purpose here is not to be graphic, but to simply reveal what our journey was really like. He had major issues with bowel movements, mostly because his organs were struggling to remain functional due to the tumors and the chemotherapy. He often could not successfully have bowel movements, or he would have uncontrollable diarrhea.

When he went to school, he often had to use his own fingers to literally dig the feces from his anus; it just wouldn't come out any other way. Another time, he called us crying because he had diarrhea and couldn't clean himself up. His roommates had to clean him up, which was no doubt a humiliating experience he would have never wanted in a million years. This loss of basic dignity was just a reality of what he faced—and another reason to marvel at the courage he displayed in wanting to stay at school or live life as fully as possible all the way to the end. It would have been so much easier to just hide away where the light of embarrassment would never find him.

When he moved back home, our daily routine with him was just as bad. The process of cleaning and repacking the three-inch bedsore on his back, which went all the way to his bone, would take more than an hour. Blood, pus, urine, mucus, saliva, and feces—these were just the things we learned to live with every day. We often had to dig the feces out of his backside for him, just to help him have some relief from the painful constipation that caused him severe suffering.

I (Tony) need to say a few things here about Kelly that she would never agree with or say about herself. You can never understand the level of care Kelly showed to Tyler throughout the entire process. She never left his side, and she always took care of anything he needed, no matter how gruesome or difficult it was.

There were many people who walked this journey with us. One of them was Tyler's palliative care nurse from Riley Children's Hospital, Amy Haskamp. She and her husband are Purdue alumni and diehard Boilermaker fans. She has become a dear friend to our family through this whole process; we love her so much. She was with us when Tyler passed—not as his nurse, but as a friend. That night, she took Kelly's mom aside and told her that she had never met a mother who had taken such good care of her child. She said that one of the main reasons Tyler lived as long as he did was because of the level of care Kelly had provided for him, as evidenced by the fact that the wound on his back never became infected even once.

Kelly was Tyler's champion from the first breath of his life to his last, letting herself be spent to the last drop of her strength for the ones she loved. As her husband, there is no adequate way to express my love and appreciation for her heart and actions toward me and our family. I want to honor her by letting the world know how amazing she is as a wife, mother, and person.

I (Kelly) am humbled by Tony's sweet words, but I know that any mother would do the same. It is who we are. I'm made to be a caretaker; and for this entire journey, I was honored to be Tyler's primary caretaker. It's just what I do. It is my purpose. Outside of being a child of God, this is just me.

Now that Tyler is no longer here to be cared for, my greatest fear is that I will lose myself. I'm worried that I will lose sight of my purpose and what I am supposed to be doing next. Yes, I know I have other children to care for, and I fully intend to keep loving them with all my heart and my service. I just mean that going from being a twenty-four-hour-a-day caretaker, trying to help my son just survive another day, to just taking one of the boys to ball practice—that is going to be a hard transition.

I faced a great deal of depression during Tyler's remission. I also know that I'm a slow processor, meaning it all comes to me later. I don't anticipate that this will be any different. This is as raw and real as I can be; the future looks very uncertain for me. I ask for your prayers because these are uncharted waters for all of us, as they are for everyone else out there in a similar situation.

Again, we say all this to help raise awareness of the needs of families facing pediatric cancer situations. Throughout our journey of discovery, we have heard that 96 percent of all funding for cancer research goes to adult research, leaving only 4 percent for children. A recent article in *The Wall Street Journal* outlines some of the reasons for the discrepancy that exists here between the two areas of research. One reason is that because there are so many fewer instances of cancer in children than adults, pediatric trials are risky and unprofitable. However, a new law now requires pharmaceutical companies to test potential cancer drugs on children as well. This law goes into effect in 2020. Companies are already ramping up, and some are planning children's trials sooner than the deadline.[4]

This is exciting news that will bring hope to families like ours. Our hope is that, unlike ours, their families will be able to beat cancer. The truth is that the choices and bad habits of adults, such as smoking, cause, or at least contribute to, some adult cancers. But children are innocent, and we want to be on the front lines of the battle to see more funding raised for more research so that not even one child will ever have to face what our Tyler faced.

And Yet . . .

So this is where we are—reality with all its ugly and confusing elements. We know that in some ways, we will always bear this deep soul ache that comes with losing a child in the way we have lost Tyler. But we also choose to believe that there is light somewhere ahead,

---

4   Lucette Lagnado, "For Children with Cancer, Hope for New Treatments," *The Wall Street Journal*, updated January 15, 2019, https://www.wsj.com/articles/for-children-with-cancer-hope-for-new-treatments-11547561004#comments_sector.

shining on the other side of this tunnel of pain and grief.

We plan on pushing ahead through counseling and honest community so that by God's grace, we might come out on the other side into whatever a healthy new normal might look like. We can't really see that far ahead right now, but we're trusting God and the people around us that it's out there somewhere.

And while we want to be real here, we also want to remind ourselves and maybe encourage you by proclaiming what keeps holding us together: "We are afflicted in every way, but not crushed; perplexed, but not driven to despair; persecuted, but not forsaken; struck down, but not destroyed" (2 Corinthians 4:8–9, ESV).

God gave us more time with our son than the doctors believed was possible. We know this was an answer to our prayers, as well as Tyler's prayer, to let his cancer be used for a divine purpose. Tyler's poor brain was not able to fully recall all the timelines and details after a certain point, which is why he made the error in an interview of saying that in September 2018, the doctors said he had only two months or so to live.

In actuality, when we were told there was a fourth tumor on his clavicle and that the tumor on his spine had more than doubled in size, the doctors did say that Tyler had anywhere from two weeks to two months to live, but that was in May 2018, not September. When he came straight home into hospice care, a nurse told us that it was probably more like days, not weeks. Things were bad enough that we called in friends and family to say their good-byes.

But somehow, Tyler just kept living when he should have been dying.

The fact that Tyler lived as long as he did was not by accident. It was a part of God's unique plan for his life—a life Tyler had fully surrendered to God. I (Tony) will never forget a talk I had with Tyler about two weeks before he died. I was lying down next to him in his bed, and we were just talking. "Dad," he said, "you know there was nothing more that I wanted to do than to just please God—and you and Mom—with my life."

I lay my head down on his and wept. I said, "Tyler, from a father's perspective, there is no greater joy than hearing your child say that he desires to please the Lord and his parents." This was my son, and despite all that we had lost, we had still gained that which matters most in this life . . . and the next. Especially toward the end of his life, our son was following in the footsteps of faith. He was a servant to people and a devoted follower of Jesus.

You might not be a person who believes, but we hope you can at least open your heart to the miracle of what God did in Tyler. He had every human reason to turn his back on Christ, but instead, his suffering just brought them closer and closer. It doesn't seem to make sense, but this is what we mean when we refer to "God's ways." They are counterintuitive to our ways, but we have learned that his grace and peace are greater than anything else.

Tyler believed that the love of Christ was better than life itself . . . he lost one, but he never lost the other for even a single moment.

I (Tony) remember advice Kelly once gave me when I was struggling with something I really wanted to happen, but that never would. She said, "Tony, this is obviously not what God has for you right now. It's just not his timing or the purpose he has for you in your life." This wisdom has helped me so many times through all of this. When we're looking at other people, we must realize that God has given them *their* purpose and path wherever they are. But God has called us to where *we* are. We can't compare or trade our lives; we just have to find the grace and the strength to make it through our own stories, accepting that God knows what he's doing with each of us.

In our situation, we faced so much, but we are overwhelmingly thankful that our son knows Jesus and that when he left this life, Jesus was right there to meet him on the other side of this thin curtain between here and there. We have been struck down, but we are not destroyed because we have discovered that in life or in death, knowing Jesus means everything.

One of our favorite movies is *It's a Wonderful Life*. If you think about it, George Bailey had a pretty tough life, between saving his brother, who had fallen through the ice, going deaf in one ear after a grief-stricken pharmacist unjustly slapped him around, constantly having to give up all his own hard-earned money to keep his credit union and his community from being overtaken by greedy landlords, and always giving up on his dreams because needy people really needed him, including his alcoholic uncle who lost the bank deposit, a loss that was going to surely put them all under.

You probably already know the story, but pretend that you have watched only the first half of the movie. You would probably wonder why in the world the movie is called "It's a *Wonderful* Life." After all, George Bailey's life seemed anything but wonderful at the film's halfway point. If you were to leave the theater during intermission, you would have the wrong opinion of the whole story. It makes sense only after the miraculous ending.

The same is true of us. Even though Tyler died, this is not the end of our story. We are mourning and grieving now, but it would be foolish to turn off the movie and assume that "it's a terrible life." There is so much more to come that we won't be able to see until the ending, when the credits roll and we see how God made the whole story work out for our good.

Our twenty-first-century cynical viewpoints of heaven keep us from seeing this reality. We feel as if what we are experiencing here now must be the best part of our existence. In fact, most Christians don't look forward to heaven because their image of it is a place where baby angels float around on clouds, and the best thing we have to look forward to is driving on streets of gold, which loses its luster after a couple of laps. We also say things like, "We'll just worship God for a million years!"—which doesn't sound like "heaven" to most people because they struggle to make it through a twenty-minute worship time in their churches each week.

But scripture paints a different picture of heaven: as a real place where we are not floating spirits or angels with harps, but where we have real bodies, real conversations with our real family and friends, real jobs and purpose, real food and drink, and real life that really goes on forever. Heaven can feel weird and unfamiliar until we see the many glimpses of heaven in scripture that most of us overlook in the modern age.[5]

Our Tyler was not a perfect kid, but we have hope in the middle of our grief because we know that he is with a perfect savior. This was

---

5   A great resource we recommend that explores many of these forgotten scriptures about heaven is a book called *Heaven* by Randy Alcorn.

the purpose of Tyler's life—to shine light on the grace that God offers to all people in every situation. Through his suffering, Tyler became *more* confident of this hope, not less. *This* was a part of the miracle that we can see, even though there was a miracle of healing we were never able to fully see. His final few years here were spent fighting against cancer, but they were also spent living courageously, speaking out about the life he had found in a relationship with Christ, and giving hope to those who are struggling to find it.

His remarkable life here, which still seems far too short to us, is over . . . but his life itself has only just begun.

So wherever you are, there is hope. That is what Tyler wanted you to know. He died, but he did not lose. His life continues to flourish in God's great plan of redemption that will someday be finished and revealed. And when it is all said and done at the end of this story—an ending we cannot yet see—we will fully realize that, despite all the pain and suffering, in Christ, it has been and will continue to be *a wonderful life*. God has blessed us with so much joy and with many special memories through the challenges of our journey. We are forever grateful that God gave us three wonderful boys, a loving community, and a purpose for living in all situations.

In the end, we will *see*—and we will *be*—the upset.

CHAPTER 23

Famous Last Words

In the last month or so of Tyler's life, he wrote two profoundly compelling articles that millions of people read and shared. They became his own famous last words. Their invaluable inclusion here is a final glimpse into the exact words this phenomenally brave young man was thinking during his final days.

These words had a profound effect on many people. In fact, on a visit to the White House with his football team to be honored for winning the national championship against Alabama, Clemson Head Coach Dabo Swinney chose to use much of his speech to share extensively about the life and legacy of Tyler Trent, quoting many times from the following article.

As I Face My Last Days, Here Is Why I Am Grateful
by Tyler Trent
Published in the *Indianapolis Star* on December 5, 2018

When I started to have trouble breathing and began convulsing the morning of September 25, I thought for sure my roommates would return to find a limp, dead body in my wheelchair.

However, after about eight minutes, my body returned to normal. Which meant I would take my morphine to battle my daily back pain from the ever-growing tumor on my spine. Without the pain medication, I was basically unable to function. So, after double-checking that I could breathe normally, I went to class.

This probably leads one to ask themselves: Why didn't you tell anyone?

One, I didn't tell anyone because I love my school and learning at Purdue University and didn't want to give that away.

Two, I didn't want to scare my family. There was already a lot of conflict and tension at home about my determination to return to Purdue this fall with the tumor on my spine, and I didn't want to add to that.

And, three, I didn't know how serious it was.

After much Googling and common sense in class, I figured out that the tumor growing on my L3 spine was causing me to slowly lose the ability to use the left side of my upper body, as well as my legs. The tumor paralyzed me from the waist down, but it wasn't until my mom back home in Carmel, Indiana, saw that I wasn't tweeting like normal that she realized something was wrong.

So when my mom and grandma came to visit and I had another seizure in front of them, my mom—out of concern, of course—insisted that I move back home. I was devastated, but deep down I knew it was the right decision. Unfortunately, the seizures were just the beginning of my medical problems.

Real-life nightmare before the Ohio State game

I was also facing issues using the restroom, and after several tests, doctors figured out that my kidneys were failing quickly, the result of almost four years of chemotherapy being pumped through my body.

In a quick turn of events for me, my doctors were telling me I had only a couple of weeks to live and that I was going to have to live with tubes manually flushing my kidneys. These tubes would turn out to be a nightmare because half the time they didn't work, and we have to manually flush saline through my kidneys to get them working again. Unfortunately, the week of the Ohio State vs. Purdue game, this is what happened:

My tubes failed, and I had to be rushed to the hospital to undergo an emergency surgery to fix them. This was done without anesthesia. It was a nightmare come true; you can feel the operation happening but can't stop it or scream out because of the pain. I have gained a new respect for veterans of war who had to undergo operations on the battlefield without modern medicine.

At this point, you may be wondering: Where's the gratitude? After all, isn't that the title of this column?

Well, yes. Yes, it is.

I still have a choice to make

I am extremely grateful that even though I had to endure that grueling pain and surgery, and later in the week spent an entire day throwing up and running a fever due to the surgery, I was able to attend that football game with my family and experience all the love and support. Not only from Purdue fans, but from across the nation, including Ohio State fans.

Though I am in hospice care and have to wake up every morning knowing that the day might be my last, I still have a choice—to make that day the best it can be. To make the most of whoever comes to visit, texts, tweets or calls me.

Yet, isn't that a choice we all have every day? After all, nobody knows the number of days we have left. Some could say we are all in hospice to a certain degree.

So why don't we act like it? Where is your gratitude? This Christmas, what are you thankful for? I had to write my will recently, and I'm just thankful I can give my family Christmas presents, maybe even for one last time. Let's not forget my doctors gave me three months to live almost two and a half months ago. So why can't we live grateful lives? Why can't we make every day count like it's the last?

To me, that's what gratitude in hospice means.

Life Can Change in a Blink—So Should Your Dreams
by Tyler Trent
Published in the *IndyStar* on December 17, 2018

Dreams: What are they?

When you were a little kid, you probably had a dream of growing up and becoming someone special. It could have been a firefighter, policeman, famous singer, or maybe, just maybe, you wanted to become the president of the United States.

We all have these big, fantastic job dreams when we are little. For me, I wanted to be a dump-truck driver. I know, I know, it probably was not the ideal choice for a six-year-old me. However, I absolutely loved dump trucks and construction videos they were in. I would spend hours upon hours in front of the TV watching construction videos on VHS.

Like most, as I grew older, my dreams changed. I can tell you with confidence that I no longer have dreams of driving a dump truck, but I do have dreams of one day graduating college, getting married, and having children.

Further down on my list of dreams, I would love to publish a book on my story and tell the world of all the amazing things the Lord has done for me. That, and attend a Cubs game at every single MLB stadium.

It is going to be a challenge figuring out which one of those last couple I should complete first . . .

The crazy thing about dreams is that they give us purpose in life, something to work toward (or procrastinate from, depending on who you are). Purpose is a universal human need, but that purpose and those dreams can be dashed away in the blink of an eye.

That sudden loss of a family member, severe illness diagnosis, loss of a job. You name it.

But why?

This is a question I have asked myself several times throughout the last few years. Why would a good, gracious, and holy God want to take away our dreams? These are not typically sinful things. I mean, who wouldn't want to spend hours upon end traveling the country to watch people hit balls with sticks?

It is because God wants us dreaming about him. All that time you have spent thinking and dreaming about the perfect summer vacation or perfect spouse? Yeah, God wants you to spend that time thinking about him and digging into his Word. Now, I am most certainly not saying that God is going to punish you for your wonderful dreams. But let's not fleece ourselves; as with technology, how much time are we spending away from the one who provides us with every breath—wondering if I will ever graduate college? Wondering if I ever will be able to publish a book or attend a Cubs game at every MLB stadium? Then the realization comes: if I was able to constantly change what I wanted to be as a little kid, why can't I do it now?

Because I certainly have been admitted into one of the best universities in the nation. I certainly have had the blessing of attending several Cubs games when many fans have yet to see one. I certainly have impacted others through Facebook and CaringBridge posts. I certainly have been declared cancer-free before.

When we change our perspective on our own dreams, we realize that it was not God who blocked those dreams. He just morphed them into his perfect plan.

—Excerpt from a book I'll probably never finish

Afterword

by Drew Brees

A s a football player, I have been blessed to be part of many unfor-gettable games and moments. A state championship at Austin (Texas) Westlake High School in 1996, a Big Ten Conference title at Purdue University in 2000, and a Super Bowl win with the New Orleans Saints in 2009 are a few that have brought great joy to me, my family, and our fans throughout my career. And who can forget the game-winning touchdown catch by Seth Morales to beat Ohio State on our road to the Rose Bowl in 2000...a moment simply known by Purdue faithful as "The Catch."

But despite these incredible moments, I can honestly say without a doubt the Purdue–Ohio State game on October 20, 2018—which I watched from a hotel room in Baltimore the night before the Saints played the Ravens—stands out as one of the greatest events I have ever seen. The Boilermakers have upset the Buckeyes on a few occasions throughout the years, but never in such convincing fashion: 49–20. And while the players on the field certainly were responsible for the victory, we *all* believe there was more to it.

Tyler Trent.

He predicted it on national television. As crazy as that sounded

(Purdue was 3–3 and unranked; Ohio State was 7–0 and ranked number 2 in the country), I think he got everybody at Purdue—players, coaches, and fans—*believing* it could happen. There definitely was divine intervention at work, and it was amazing. A testament to the power of faith and the human spirit.

It truly was "The Upset."

Tyler was unbelievable, and not because of his bold prediction. The impact he had on the Purdue football team, the entire university, and people all over the country was nothing short of inspiring.

Although I did not have the opportunity to meet Tyler, I certainly felt like I knew him. We shared a common love for Purdue and its athletics teams. I first heard about Tyler in September 2017. He camped out outside Ross-Ade Stadium the night before the Boilermakers played Michigan to be one of the first students to enter and get a prime seat. Nothing particularly unique about that—there were other like-minded students camping out that night. But I think it's safe to say Tyler was the only Boilermaker fan there who had undergone chemotherapy just hours before.

This display of passion for Purdue led Tyler to forge a relationship with head coach Jeff Brohm and his players, who ultimately named him an honorary team captain. And there was Tyler, at midfield for games against Nebraska in 2017 and Northwestern in 2018, taking part in the coin toss for the Boilermakers' annual Hammer Down Cancer Games.

The morning of the 2018 Ohio State game, ESPN *College Game-Day* featured Tyler, and it elevated his story nationwide. As it did to so many viewers, whether they were Purdue fans or not, it brought tears to our eyes. For someone so young to display such a positive spirit and possess such an unwavering faith was remarkable.

As part of the story, Purdue quarterback David Blough was asked how Tyler looked in the late stages on his ongoing battle with osteosarcoma. David's response was equally beautiful and poignant: "He looks like a Boilermaker. He looks like somebody who is going to fight until there is no fight."

From a local story to national news, Tyler enthusiastically used his adversity as a platform to increase awareness for pediatric cancer and to raise money for cancer research. It never was about Tyler and his challenges—it was about doing whatever he could to make the world a better place.

He did that many times over.

Tyler inspired countless people with his strength and his will. Fittingly, he received the 2018 Disney Spirit Award as college football's most inspirational figure. In a room full of the game's top players and coaches, Tyler clearly was the star of the show on that December night in Atlanta, receiving a standing ovation from the audience and certainly warming more hearts among those watching on television.

Let's not forget Tyler's family. As a husband and a father to four children, I can't imagine the emotional roller coaster they undoubtedly experienced over the past year and a half. They, too, are an inspiration. Tyler Trent never will be forgotten. But our thoughts also are with Tony, Kelly, Blake, and Ethan forever. God brings people into our lives, whether directly or indirectly, to show us the power of love, courage, and faith. The Trent family embodies this. We are all better for having them in our lives.

#TylerStrong
Boiler Up!

Epilogue

The In-Betweens of Sadness and Celebration

(Reflections from Family and Friends Who Knew and Loved Tyler)

What Tyler Wanted

It had not come as a surprise, but the death of Tyler Trent still produced a shockwave that reverberated throughout Purdue, the state of Indiana, and the entire nation. His dream to leave a legacy was coming true, even as he had to abandon his dream of defeating cancer in his lifetime. His family and friends began the process of grieving their loss, a process that was only getting started.

This epilogue captures some of their thoughts during these difficult moments, dividing them into two main sections. The first section is an essay written by Blake Trent, and the second captures many perspectives from Tyler's friends and family at his memorial service.

Part 1
Harsh Reality
(An Essay by Blake Trent)

What do you think about when you hear the word "cancer"? What images come to mind as you process that word? For me, it means something different from what it would for most.

As an eighteen-year-old writing this, the word "cancer" is a double-edged sword because I think about all the things my brother taught me as a result of his sickness. I think about all the horrible things that it did to him. I think about the ways in which God worked throughout his life and used him for greatness. I think about everything and analyze every detail. My mind is always working and pondering what will happen next.

That's why, when my parents sat me down in their room one evening in July 2014 with a stone-cold look on their faces, my heart was already racing as I pondered what it could be that they were about to tell me. I could feel the adrenaline spreading throughout my body like a flame following a trail of gasoline as they laid it on me for the first time: my brother had a "rare form of bone cancer." At the time, I could never have guessed what this would mean to me, or what this journey over the past five years would look like, but one thing was for certain: I was in for a ride.

As time went on and so did the hospital visits, fourteen-year-old me didn't really know what to think. This was a whole new experience, a whole new side of life that I had never seen before. I was introduced to the side of life that says, "This can happen to you and to the people you love without warning—and there's nothing you can do about it." At least, that's how it felt to me in the moment as I walked down those white marble halls, feeling a sense of emptiness wash over me.

Don't get me wrong; seeing my brother was the most important thing I could do, but every time I was in that hospital over those five years, it was a reminder. That hospital reminded me of all the things that were wrong in my life, and that my brother was sick and there was a chance that he might not make it out alive.

This harsh reality makes one have a certain view of the world.

Either you think that life is good or you think that it's not. For me personally, having all this happen at the ripe young age of fourteen, I started to view life as a dark place with many negative aspects. This time in my life was the first I can remember the depression starting. I can remember this being the defining factor because it wasn't until I was presented with the sobering fact that my brother had a rare and aggressive form of bone cancer that I started to truly think about what can happen in life. I was opened up to life's unfair and unseen circumstances. The difference here is that my unforeseen circumstance was one that no fourteen-year-old should ever have to face.

Fast-forward two years: now we're at the beginning of my sophomore year of high school. My brother had been recently deemed cancer-free for the first and last time, but my depression still did not waver. Susceptible as ever, this was also the year I started my first public school experience. I wasn't talking to anyone about my depression—not because I didn't want to, but because I didn't really know how and because I was genuinely afraid to.

As a male in a society that can be extremely deconstructive, I began believing that "guys don't cry." To me, showing any true emotion as a male in this environment was a sign of weakness, and people will thrive off of your vulnerability. That's one thing I learned very quickly. As time went on, so did my depression and lack of support system.

I had so much family right next to me, willing to help me if I ever needed it. I had God right there by my side, but I was too nervous to ask, and I wasn't choosing my family at the time. I was choosing my friends. I was choosing them because I wanted to feel happy, even though they weren't the ones who were really going to be there for me. I wanted to just *feel*—because it was almost like I didn't even know how to feel anymore.

So I eventually turned to drugs. I chose to do something I knew I shouldn't do, even with the very present fact that I could receive help whenever I wanted. I was so caught up within myself and within the depression that was taking hold of every freed thought in my mind that drugs seemed like the way to go.

I wasn't really addicted to the drugs; I was addicted to the fact that I could "leave" the negative space of my mind and escape to somewhere else. I could go somewhere else for a while and be comfortable.

"Comfortable" was exactly how it felt for me, and that's all I wanted, because it felt like every single day, all I wanted to do was jump out of my own skin. I didn't do drugs to fit in or to "look cool" to others; I did it because I was so unhappy with myself that I wanted to be someone else.

I genuinely started to hate life, and ironically, the drugs helped me get to this place faster. It was a vicious cycle because without any support from others, I was trying to cure myself. I felt depressed until I did drugs, and then I would feel okay for a while. Then I would go back to feeling depressed again because I was trying to fill a hole inside of me that had been there since a young age.

Drugs gave me a false sense of hope that I was going to be okay—until they wore off and I realized that I had been lied to. But I kept doing the drugs anyway. I didn't stop because I didn't feel like I had a fallout plan. I didn't have anyone to help me with my problems because I never told anyone about them in the first place. I didn't even think to ask, and I didn't even think to rely on the only person who could even save me from the dark place I was in: God.

Eventually, my parents caught on to what I was doing. I got into pretty big trouble, but even that didn't stop me. I was faced with the very demeaning fact that not only was I doing drugs, but I was also actively hiding it from my parents—because now they were watching me closely. The stress and pressure it put on me to get away with it, combined with the fact that I had a brother whose cancer had come back, was not easy to handle.

I eventually convinced my parents to trust me again, but I went right back out and broke their trust again. Don't get me wrong; there were many times that I would genuinely try to stop and do "normal" things that didn't require being high. But inevitably, I would just end up getting depressed and would go back to my negative ways. I kept on actively destroying my life for a while, and in the moment, it seemed like a great idea—it always does until you take too many drugs.

That's exactly what I did. I took too many drugs and talked to God, literally. I'm not talking about some drug-induced vision that happened as a direct result of taking the drugs. I was having anxiety attacks, muscle spasms, cramps, psychotic episodes, and a host of all sorts of horrible physical and mental symptoms from what I had taken that night. Regardless of what I was feeling, there was one crystal clear, sovereign moment I had while struggling through all this that I will never forget.

God spoke to me, and he played visions before my eyes of what my life would look like if I continued down this path. But he also showed me what it would look like if I chose to follow him and live according to his will. In the midst of what was one of the most challenging times in my life, he sought me out and gave me direction; and I realized in that moment that I had a choice to make. I could continue taking drugs and waste my life by diverting my focus, or I could follow God and live out the true purpose that he has for me.

The next morning, I woke up, and the memories from the night before flooded back into my consciousness. I made a choice in that moment to change my life. Some of you might be reading this and thinking, *What? There's no way that really happened! Clearly, the visions you were having were because of the drugs and your altered state of consciousness.*

To those people, I say, believe what you must. But one thing is true: I know the difference between a drug-induced vision and a sovereign, holy, immortal God reaching his hand out and providing me with the guidance that I desperately needed. Only God could have done that, because the night before, God had been the furthest thing from my mind; but when I woke up the next morning, he was the first thing I thought about.

Being the brother of a cancer patient is never easy, and will never be for anyone. I share my experiences in hopes that others could get a glimpse of what it's like, because others should know of the challenges that will be faced for everyone involved. I was forced to face a reality that I was too young to understand. As a result, I grew up facing challenges that I could never be prepared to face, and I asked myself questions that kids should never have to ask themselves.

Extraordinarily, my brother's cancer was the outlet where Tyler taught me what it means to be a God-fearing man. My brother showed me what it means to fight and how to have faith and hope, no matter the circumstance. He taught me things that I will carry with me every single day and for the rest of my life. Most importantly,

Tyler showed me God; and through Tyler's struggles, God used Tyler to prove to me that the "hole" I have felt inside of me for as long as I can remember is simply what life feels like without the presence of the only true savior.

Because of my savior—the one my brother trusted in and taught me to trust in—I left that life of searching for meaning and wholeness in drugs and everything else that lifestyle offers. I found it to be empty, so I have no need to go back to it. Even though I can't hug my brother today, his legacy is still hugging me. He gave me the best gift a brother could ever have: the hope that only Christ can give. Though I miss him so much, I am forever grateful. I miss you so much, Tyler. Love you, my brother.

Part 2
Celebrating the Life of Tyler Trent
(Reflections from Family and Friends)

As Tyler's family and community prepared for his memorial service, they were keenly aware of the challenges such an event would produce. After all, millions of people had followed his story because of the ESPN piece and the hundreds of other media stories, not to mention dozens of high-profile media and political personalities who could participate.

A statistician to the very end, Tyler had met with two of his pastors, Mark Vroegop and Joe Wittmer, to plan many of the elements of the event. He knew exactly what he wanted for his service, from the songs that would be sung to the verses and messages that would be shared. The stage was decorated with all the sports awards, jerseys, and memorabilia that had completely covered the walls of Tyler's makeshift hospital room in the dining room of his Carmel home. So this service truly was a celebration of his life, as well as the exact story and message that Tyler most wanted to leave as his legacy.

This second part of the epilogue attempts to capture some of the sentiments shared at his service, although obviously, the nearly three-hour event contained far too many stories, speakers, and insights to include them all. The purpose is to let you become even more acquainted with Tyler, his story, and his faith as you see each of these through the eyes of a few people who knew him and loved him best. Many new elements of Tyler's story are revealed in their heartfelt reflections.

But the fact that this memorial section of the epilogue does not include everything that was said at the event is not meant to diminish anyone's value or the value of what they shared. Please know that if someone or something is not included here or has been edited down, it is simply because there is not enough space and time for the entire experience to be captured in its entirety. You can view Tyler's entire service on YouTube.[6]

Influence at the Highest Level

Vice President Mike Pence was scheduled to be in attendance at Tyler's service, but last-minute circumstances in Washington, DC, altered his ability to make the trip. He sent a letter instead that Indiana Governor Eric Holcomb read:

> Dear Trent family, our hearts are heavy—with yours—over the loss of Tyler, and we send our deepest condolences as you grieve his passing.
>
> Tyler touched the hearts of our nation and he continually built up others, even in the midst of his own battle with osteosarcoma. When we spoke with Tyler not long ago, we were moved by his passion for God's Word and his commitment to Jesus Christ. We will never forget the depth of his faith. His courage and conviction have left an indelible mark on us, much as they have among our home congregation of College Park Church and across the state of Indiana—and the nation.
>
> As Americans across the country have witnessed, Tyler's determination to live life to its fullest empowered him to lead in the fight against pediatric cancer with the Riley Hospital for Children and carry the mantle of "Purdue's biggest fan," inspiring his beloved Boilermakers to their

---

6   The full video of Tyler's celebration service is available at https://www.your-church.com/remembering-tyler-trent/

historic victory over Ohio State!

The Bible tells us, "A good name is more desirable than great riches," and Tyler leaves behind a good name that will remain in the hearts of the countless people he touched. Our lives are richer because of his, and through his courageous example, he truly showed us all what it means to be "Tyler Strong!"

As you mourn Tyler's loss, yet look to the hope of a heavenly reunion, please be assured of our prayers for God to comfort and carry you in this difficult time.

With deepest sympathies, Michael R. Pence, Vice President of the United States, and Karen Pence, Second Lady of the United States

Governor Holcomb then continued with his own sentiments.

Janet and I certainly echo what the vice president said in his letter. The entire state of Indiana—and beyond—was incredibly touched by Tyler's story and was inspired by his courage, his bravery, and—most importantly—his faith and his love.

In this new and next season, Purdue has a mighty and a powerful "sixth man" cheering them on this year! Tony and Kelly, we do know that for those who walk in the Lord's path, good-byes are never forever. We'll keep praying for you and the entire family until we're all reunited in his kingdom!

Batman and Robin

The next gentleman to take the podium was Gregg Doyel, a sports journalist for the *IndyStar*. Through his moving words, he honored Tyler with the razor-sharp wit the two had shared in their many conversations, along with a unique, sometimes humorous perspective of the uncanny way Tyler's story and message had constantly been elevated in the hearts of the nation.

Hi, I'm Gregg Doyel. I write for the *Indianapolis Star*,

and the reason I'm telling you that is, that's why I know Tyler—a great young sportswriter at Purdue, eager to get better! We talked about writing and went from there. And, for that, I want to thank Tony and Kelly for opening the doors to your home to me.

And when I'm there, I'm watching. As you guys know, I'm always watching, and I see the strength, the courage, and the faith that you showed Tyler. You are the wind in that little angel's wings! And he was in the wind in ours, wasn't he? We could not get enough of Tyler Trent! And it's because, while he had cancer, he wasn't just taking it; he wasn't just dying. That kid was living! His life. His choices.

One of the last things he did was the Music City Bowl. He went there with Purdue. And yes, he went to the game, but he went to the functions around the game as well. And you should have seen the folks lined up—adults, strangers—lined up to meet Tyler Trent. To shake his hand. To get a picture with him.

Somehow, this homeschooled kid from Carmel became a Beatle! And because he could have that impact on folks, sports figures around the country were watching. And they noticed—and they wanted Tyler to know, "I see you! We're inspired by you. We're fighting with you!"

And so, to visit Tyler regularly was to see his room look like what you're seeing up here, which is to say, his room looked like a sports memorabilia store! Vinatieri. Andrew Luck. I mean, Drew Brees. Just amazing!

You never knew what you'd see in his room, whether it was a card from Steve Alford or Dabo Swinney or the jerseys poppin' up left and right. You never knew what you'd hear in there, either. So one time, the phone rings and Tyler answers. I hear the voice coming from the cell phone, and I think I recognize it. I'm in there with Grandma and—sure enough—Tyler hangs up and says, "Well, that was Kevin Pritchard of the Pacers. Wanted to know if I'll be the honorary team president this season." So me and Grandma, at this point, we roll our eyes. Of course that just happened!

Another time, there was a knock on the door. Tony goes and answers it. He talks to a few people on the porch, comes back inside, and says, "Tyler, that was a young woman from the neighborhood." He says, "Y'all don't know each other, but she's at Kansas now, running track and cross-country. That was her and some of her teammates at the door. They signed a card for you. They want you to know that they've been watching you; they're inspired by you—in Kansas! And they wanted to bring this card."

And so, Grandma—that's another eye-roll for us. Of course that just happened!

One more. The phone rings, and Tyler answers, "Hello?"

The voice says, "Tyler, this is Mike."

"Mike who?"

Governor Holcomb stole my thunder already, but the voice says, "This is Mike Pence." Mike Pence was just making a phone call to Tyler Trent. These things would happen, and Tyler would say, "It's crazy!" He loved it; it *was* crazy.

He knew he had a platform that kids like him—kids with cancer—don't get. He earned it, but this doesn't happen. So he wasn't just fighting for himself; he was fighting for kids all over the country—he knew he was—he was fighting for kids who haven't been diagnosed with cancer yet. I hate saying the word "yet" because maybe it won't happen.

Tyler was doing this to the point that Riley researchers asked him, "Can we cultivate some of your cells and call it the T^2 line of cells? We want to study your tumor." And at great personal cost. Tyler knew that it was gonna hurt; he knew the process.

But he did it. And if someone could tell the future and tell me that in five years we're going to have a cure for cancer, and that it's going to come from a T^2 line of cells—that there was a cure for cancer and that Tyler Trent did that—after what I've seen for the past year, I'd say, "Sounds about right!"

You can tell a lot about somebody by the things they choose to talk about. Tony and Kelly, I never told you this, but here goes. Tyler chose to talk about his brothers to me. And through Tyler—through his words—where are you, Ethan? I know you. Jock. Football player. Mischievous little imp! Photo-bombing maestro! Tyler would compare you to (and in this room, a lot of you guys are going to get this, especially one of you), Tyler would compare your larger-than-life personality to Brady Brohm. There you go.

And Blake. Quiet, introspective, brilliant Blake. Going to be a pilot. So artistically gifted that no one knows what he's better at: creating with his hands or the written word. To hear Tyler tell it, the most talented writer in this room is you, Blake. Standing up here, I'm not sure how I feel about that!

Nah, I know exactly how I feel about it. I love it! I love it, and frankly, I'm used to it. To be in Tyler's sphere was to be delightfully overshadowed at every turn. He wrote for the *Star*, actually, for the past month or so. And when I got hired four years ago, they told me, "This is a one-sports-columnist paper—and you're the one." Well, Tyler writes, the work gets published, and he updates his Twitter bio with "*Indy Star* sports columnist." And then there were two.

Of those two, I know the hierarchy here. Tyler was Batman, and I'll be your Robin. Yet, better than Batman, Tyler was Superman—and if that makes me Aquaman, so be it. I was reminded of it all the time—delightfully so!

Last month, I was at a basketball game at Purdue. They beat Maryland. I've been here for four years, and this has never happened before. After the game, Matt Painter does his press conference and then makes a beeline for me. I see him coming, and I think, "It's about time! I see you coming, Matt Painter. Come along!"

Matt comes up to me, puts his hand on my shoulder, and says, "How's Tyler?" He wanted to talk about Tyler, and that's what we did.

That happened all the time. All the time! It's happening even now. Tyler died the night of January 1. That night, I wrote a story in the *Star*, a tribute to Tyler, and put it online. The next morning, I get a phone call from area code 765. I don't know it, but I answer it anyway. A woman says, "Call from the office of Mitch Daniels [the president of Purdue University]. Hold, please. He'd like to speak with you." Mitch wanted to speak about the tribute—he wanted to speak about Tyler. This was twelve hours after, and we were all raw and hurting at this point. But I allowed myself a little smile because I'm thinking, "Only you, Tyler Trent, can get a sportswriter like me a phone call from the past governor of Indiana and the president of Purdue. Only you, Superman!"

So in closing, I've called Tyler a few things here tonight. Superman and Batman and a Beatle. I've got one more. I'm going to steal this from David Blough and what he told Tom Rinaldi on that ESPN story that ran the morning of the Ohio State game. At one point, Tom looks at David and says, "You visit Tyler. When you visit him, what do you see?"

Well, I'm watching the show in my home in Greenwood, and I know the Trents are watching it in Carmel. Grandma and Kelly had the same reaction I had. I know because we've talked about this.

Our reaction to that question was, "'What do you see?' Tyler's losing weight; he's losing his hair! What do you mean, 'What do you see?' What kind of question is that? How do you answer that?" Well, Tom wasn't asking me that question—thank goodness! He was asking David Blough.

And Blough smiles. There are photos of David and Tyler all over the place, maybe some around here. You've seen that smile David always gives Tyler—and the sun is shining on Tyler's face when David smiles at him. David smiles and he says, "I see a Boilermaker."

And so, in closing, I say, Boiler-up, Superman! I know where you're going. I know where you are. Boiler-up, Tyler! Thank you.

Two Friends in the Fray

Many friends spoke during Tyler's service, sharing childhood perspectives and stories. However, two friends in particular, Trey Mock and David Blough, offered unique and moving insights into Tyler's life in terms of his passion and mission as an adult. These two friends often choked back the tears and emotions as they honored the friend they had come to love so deeply.

Trey was the first one to share.

My name is Trey Mock, and I'm the mascot for the Indianapolis Colts. I tell you that because that's how I met Tyler. I went over to his house on March 12th of last year. I was supposed to make an appearance as Blue, take a picture, and share a few laughs. I was so inspired by his attitude that I did something I never do: I took off my mascot head, sat down, and had a conversation with Tyler. I asked questions, and I listened to his story.

I heard about his battle with cancer in his arm and then his remission. Then he told me how the cancer came back in his hip. Tyler said that when he was diagnosed with cancer the second time, he realized something. He said, "I didn't use my first fight with cancer to glorify God, and I wasn't gonna make that mistake again." The day I met him, he wasn't battling cancer for the first time or the second; this was his third time battling cancer.

He quoted one of his favorite Bible verses, a verse that you'll see on a lot of bracelets in this room tonight—1 Thessalonians 5:16–18: "Rejoice always, pray continually, give thanks in all circumstances; for this is God's will for you in Christ Jesus." I was in awe of his faith in God!

Cancer had attacked his body for the third time—and he wasn't flinching.

It didn't take long for us to become dear friends. We spent most of our time talking. We discussed everything from sports, movies, and life—to our faith. One hot day in August, we had a forty-five-minute debate on which gas station had the best Icee! After he won the argument, I drove to the Speedway gas station off 32 and purchased two large Icees.

Upon returning, we sipped on our drinks in victory and began another conversation. Tyler said with a smile, "I've decided to go back to Purdue in the fall." There were no more treatment options for Tyler's cancer; he was going to die. And still he made the decision to go back to school. I asked him why he wanted to go back, and he grabbed a book that was next to his bed.

The book was titled *When Breath Becomes Air*. It's about a doctor who's facing terminal cancer. Tyler opened the book to page 149 and read this passage: "Why? Because I could! Because that's who I was. Because I would have to learn to live a different way, seeing death as an imposing visitor but knowing that, even if I'm dying, until I actually die, I'm still living."

Tyler made a decision to live. Even if he was dying, he was going to live his life to the fullest, and I was happy for him. We circled September 30 on the calendar. It was a home game for the Indianapolis Colts against the Houston Texans. He promised to come back into town so he could work with me on our mascot program. I was so excited for that day to come.

Then two days before, I received a phone call from Tony. I could hear the sadness in his voice as he told me, "If you want to see Tyler, you need to come now." I rushed over to see him, and it didn't look good. He was in a lot of pain. As he wiped away his tears, he asked me, "We still good for the game?"

I told him not to worry about it, but he reassured me

he would be there. "A promise is a promise!" he said. Honestly, I didn't think he was going to make it through the night, and I definitely didn't think he was going to make it to the game; but in Tyler fashion, he found the strength to be on the sidelines with me that day.

After the game, he asked if I would pray with him. He knew that God had something more for him. You could see it in his eyes—everyone could. His prayer was for God to remove every obstacle so he could share his story with the world—the story of his fight against cancer and his testimony for God. We prayed, and then he said with a huge grin, "Guess where I'm headed next? To see Purdue beat Ohio State!"

The game was three weeks away. Not many people thought he would live to see it, but I wasn't doubting him anymore. And we all know how that ended. Tyler prayed for a platform, and God answered his prayer. He used his national platform to raise money for cancer research. Tyler's *goal* was to cure cancer, but his *mission* was to use his fight to glorify God.

I had the privilege to be with Tyler in the last days of that mission. I traveled with Tyler and his family to the Music City Bowl to watch his Purdue Boilermakers. Osteosarcoma is very painful, and being moved from his bed to his wheelchair was excruciating for Tyler. He made that transfer several times during that trip, back and forth between his bed and wheelchair, each time worse than the last.

The morning of the game, he sat in his wheelchair. As pain coursed through his body and tears streamed down his face, he said, "I don't know if I can do this!"

His sweet mother, Kelly, bent down to give him a kiss, and she whispered, "Tyler, I love you. I know this is your dream—to make it to the game—but we don't have to go. You don't have to prove anything to anyone." The room fell silent as we cried and lifted up prayers for Tyler.

Then Tyler spoke: "God is good all the time, and all the

time, God is good!" He lifted his head and said, "Let's do this!"

One last time, Tyler Trent rolled into a stadium of fans chanting his name. I wondered if the fans understood the moment. When Stuart Scott accepted the Jimmy V award, he said, "When you die, it does not mean you lose to cancer. You beat cancer by how you live while you live and in the manner of which you live." Tyler loved Stewart Scott, and he loved that speech.

I thought about those words as I watched the fans of the Music City Bowl cheer for Tyler. Even as he was dying, he lived his life. Tyler lived his life the way God wanted him to, and he inspired all of us every step of the way.

Two months ago, Tyler told me that this day would come, and he asked if I would speak here today. I was honored by the gesture, and I asked him what he wanted people to know. Without any hesitation, he said, "Tell them it wasn't about me. It was all about God!"

I listened to those words with tears in my eyes. He saw me struggling to fight those tears back, and he said, "It's gonna be okay, bro! Remember, either way, I win! I'm either in heaven with Jesus, or I'm here on Earth with the ones I love!"

Tyler, you won, bro. You won! And I'll always love you. Boiler-up, brother! Hammer down.

David Blough, quarterback for the Purdue Boilermakers, came to the podium next.

My name is David Blough. I am a member of the Purdue University football team and one of Tyler's co-captains. And that's the truth. Mr. and Mrs. Trent, thank you for allowing me to stand up here and share this evening as we celebrate Tyler's grace-filled life.

The forty-eight hours I got to spend with the Trent family, as a part of Tyler's entourage—like everybody else has mentioned—at the College Football Awards Show was easily the best forty-eight hours of my life. We got to do some incredible things. Hanging out with Ethan and Blake, it was all about flying on the private jet and staying at a pretty sweet hotel. We even got to meet some of our favorite sports icons.

However, what made the time I got to spend as an adopted member of the Trent family special was the conversations that were had, the relationships that were deepened, and the memories that we shared.

I think if Tyler and I would have had the opportunity to discuss what I was planning on sharing this evening, the conversation would be simple. He would want it to revolve around the five-letter word—the five-letter name—that has stood the test of time. He'd want tonight to be all about Jesus. And as we reflect on our family member, our friend, our teammate, our captain, our classmate, and our cancer-fighting warrior, most importantly tonight, we get to remember Tyler as a follower of Jesus.

It encouraged me to see Tyler in his element, cheering on his beloved Boilermakers. It inspired me to see how he relentlessly advocated for cancer research. But his undeniable love for the Lord is what has impacted my life forever. Whether it was an encouraging text he sent with scripture, one of his favorite sermons, his willingness to share his powerful testimony, or those three verses that he lived by in 1 Thessalonians, it was evident who he belonged to and who he lived for.

Psalm 23, verse 4, says, "Even though I walk through the valley of the shadow of death, I will fear no evil, for you are with me; your rod and your staff, they comfort me." Tyler sent this verse to me twice via text and, reflecting on it now, that's exactly what he was doing—walking through the valley of the shadow of death, staring it right in the face.

But because of his hope and trust in Jesus Christ, he didn't lose hope himself. He was able to see the circumstances in front of him as an opportunity to serve others—and if that's not Christ-like, I don't know what is. So, thank you, Tyler, for fighting the good fight and keeping the faith. Love you, brother!

Family Ties

Many members of the Trent family walked to the stage to support Tyler's uncle, Todd Trent, in speaking about his nephew.

Good evening. My name is Todd Trent. I am Tyler's uncle and Tony's brother. I was asked to speak about Tyler on behalf of the Trent family. It will be hard to express all I want to say in a short period of time, but I'll do my best.

Recently, someone asked, "What's different about Tyler? There are thousands of kids suffering with cancer in hospitals all over the world. Why is he getting all this attention?" I had to ponder those questions in my heart for some time. Was it his passion for sports? No, many kids are sports fanatics. Was it his "Trent stubbornness" and determination? Maybe, but there has to be more.

Was it his lovable personality that we, as a family, have adored since his birth? Probably not just that. Was it the fact that he was brilliantly smart and almost aced his SATs? Or what about all the money that is being raised for cancer research and Riley Hospital? Or was it his proclaiming love of our Lord Jesus Christ, even during his worst suffering? No, many have done that, too.

You see, Tyler was special because God gave him a specific purpose. He gave him a perfect platform to proclaim the name of Jesus Christ, and Tyler used it beautifully. Tyler used his suffering and turned it into something amazing.

God has a plan for each one of our lives. God gives us the opportunity each day to be Tyler Strong. Will we have the opportunity to affect millions of people? Probably not. But still, if we can bring only one person to Jesus Christ, we are living Tyler Strong.

My sister, Tricia, works as a nurse. She saw a man in the waiting room with a Tyler Strong T-shirt on. She went up to the gentleman and thanked him for buying one. She explained that half the proceeds went to cancer research. The man responded by saying that Tyler had changed his life. He went on to say, "I was an atheist, and Tyler restored my faith." That's amazing, just amazing.

We, like Tyler, have to choose to live life to its fullest. To make the most out of each day. To rejoice always, to pray continually, and to thank God in all circumstances. No matter what God gives us in life, it is our platform, and our opportunity, to be Tyler Strong and to be a light to a dark world.

Tyler had many beautiful words to keep in our hearts. As Tyler mentioned once, everyone has a story—there just needs to be someone to listen to it. How often do we truly take the time to listen to others and their stories? Jesus tells us to bear one another's burdens.

Tyler also said once, "We all have our own cancer, whether it be figuratively or literally. We all have problems. We all have something that is eating away at our lives. The choice is ours—to let it destroy us or to use the opportunity for good."

God tells us in Romans 8:28 that all things work together for the good to those who love God. So are our cancers or problems good? No, absolutely not. But God can use them for good.

Just look at Tyler's life. Was it a good life? Absolutely! What Tyler experienced in the last three months of his life is more than most people will experience in their lifetimes.

Tyler was given the incomprehensible diagnosis of cancer not once, twice, but three times! Each time he was diagnosed, it brought him closer to Jesus. Each time, Tyler surrendered his heart more and more to God's will and plan for his life. Jesus wants that for us—to totally trust and depend on him, and him alone. And when we totally surrender ourselves to our Lord Jesus Christ, we can all be Tyler Strong!

Let your light so shine before men that they may see

your good works and glorify your Father, which is in heaven. So, our beloved Tyler, let us continue your legacy by spreading the love of Jesus to others. We will miss you dearly, but we know you are in the arms of Jesus—no more suffering, no more tears, no more cancer. This is not goodbye; it's see you later.

And one more thing, Tyler: one, four, three. You see, in his last days, Tyler communicated by saying (with his fingers), "One, four, three," meaning "I love you."

Best Friends

Throughout his story, Tyler often reflected on a few friends who stuck by him through the rises and falls in his difficult story. Three of these friends—Josh Seals, Anni Osborne, and Josh Heinzman—shared their perspectives of Tyler, followed by his college roommate, John Kruse. They shared, one after another, beginning with Josh Seals.

Hi, I'm Josh Seals; I'm a lifelong friend of Tyler's. I've known him since he was born. We've gone to the same church and the same school, grew up in the same neighborhood, and even played on the same Little League team. Over the years, we've been through a lot of different things together, but the past few years have definitely been the richest.

The point of the service is that we want you guys to walk away smiling in remembrance of Tyler's life. And that's what I want to share with you today—just a few things that, when I think about Tyler, I just can't help but smile.

One of them is that we did a backpacking trip a few years back, after he had just beat cancer for the first time. He had a titanium arm, and he was backpacking! I was actually in the back with Blake, struggling to keep up, and he was up there—you know Tyler—and he was just getting it! He was backpacking with like thirty pounds on his backpack. Incredible.

He would tell stories each night that would make us laugh and also make us scared. Sometimes I was so scared that I didn't even want to close my hammock! Honestly. That's just how I remember it—and I love that memory.

You guys probably all know about how we chose to camp out for the Michigan game. It's an incredible story, but I think what makes it even more incredible is that while I was setting up the tent, he was getting chemotherapy. He suffered through that process, but instead of taking a sick day like most of us would, he was like, "No, we're going to go and have this incredible time!"

And that was the thing that started all this—this platform for him. His spirit was behind that from the very beginning. One of the biggest smiles comes from just remembering that night. Probably the reason it stands out and is so popular is because it's the perfect example of what I most admire about Tyler. I most admire that, while I was setting up that tent, he wouldn't give up. Even through the hardest things to endure in this life, he chose to never let them stop him. That hope was contagious and is the reason why Tyler Trent is a household name today.

It's not by chance that Tyler inspired millions. That doesn't just happen on accident. It's an intentional choice that he made every day that inspires me to my core—and it should inspire you. The world needed Tyler and was attracted to Tyler, not because of his hope, but rather who he had hope in—Christ. This world desperately needs Christ, and Tyler's life showed us just how magnificently God can use a life if you just hope in him.

It's incredible—and I'm so, so happy for you, Tyler. Like, I miss you a lot, but I have only experienced Christ just a little bit on this earth, and it's been the best thing that has ever happened to me—the most joyous days of my life! And knowing that you're in the presence of my Father right now, fully experiencing that, brings so much joy to my heart. I can't wait to be there with you. Love you!

Anni Osborne (speaking for herself and her brother, Noah Osborne) spoke next.

My name is Anni Osborne, and I'm honored to share with you some words from me and from my brother, Noah, who can't be here tonight. They're about one of my absolute dearest friends in the world. And I knew that no matter the day, the time—no matter what—he would always be there to take care of me.

Noah and I talked about this. How do you begin to summarize someone's life into a few words? You could start with what everybody saw: a twenty-year-old cancer-fighter with a whole lot of faith who worked to be a college student and a super-fan.

You could talk about what those closer to him saw: a resilient follower of Christ who embraced every situation he was put in and turned it around into something wonderful. But, to me, Tyler was a role model. I can remember sitting next to him at work one day, thinking, *The world is not ready for Tyler Trent! He is going to do something amazing—and I can't wait to sit back and one day say, "I know him!"*

Today is that day.

I've grown up watching him learn and grow and face challenges. If he didn't understand something, he would not rest until he understood it. If he didn't feel confident in something, he would work until he mastered it. If he did not agree with something, he challenged it until he agreed with it or found resolution.

Then he got cancer—and I held my breath for how it would alter my friend. It did two things: it destroyed his body, and it deepened his faith. He began to believe, with all that he had, in his savior, wanting to share the hope he found in the depths of his suffering with anyone who would listen.

I got to see him triumph, and I got to see him humbled by wave upon wave upon wave of cancer. All the while, he leaned harder into the Lord and drew upon a hope that gave him strength that defied all reason—the strength that has attracted many of the audience today.

His goal was to leave a legacy, but not his own. He wanted people to think about how Christ worked in him. He wanted people to see more than Tyler Trent, more than just a cancer-fighter; he wanted people to see God.

And through these twenty years, we were blessed to have him, and we saw it. We saw God in him! There was a hope that was not rooted in anything here but was focused on eternity—and it touched all of us. I hope you'll leave here tonight knowing that Tyler is finally free—and it is now our turn to live like Tyler did, focused on loving others and making every moment count. If we can do that, Tyler's example will live on and continue to change lives, causing others to look to our savior. I love you, Tyler!

Jake Heinzman was the next to come to the podium.

Good evening. My name is Jake Heinzman. Tonight, I want to celebrate the life of my friend, Tyler, by sharing some of our lifelong history to help you see three things about him: another side of his outgoing personality, a lesson he learned, and a prayer for those he loved best.

I can't remember a time when I didn't know Tyler. We met each other shortly after I was born—when his parents brought him to the hospital to welcome me to the world. We grew up together, played at the same preschool, shared the same church and small group, and attended high school in this very building with a graduating class of fourteen students.

We traveled the world together on mission trips to destinations such as Nicaragua and China. When it came time to choose the next step on the path of our lives, we both chose to attend Purdue University.

I want to share another side of Tyler, one that wasn't always visible in the spotlight that shone brightly over him in the last year. Tyler was hilarious! We spent countless hours laughing over board games with our friends. Tyler and I were notorious among our classmates for our odd bantering and corny jokes.

Our high school had an annual competition each fall to see who could come up with the most creative partner costumes for our Dynamic Duo Day. Tyler and I won every year, dressing as Google Maps pins, Bob Ross and a painting of a tree, and Bill and Hillary Clinton—and I do not have to tell you who was Hillary, because it was Tyler.

I believe Tyler embodied Philippians 1:21: "To live is Christ and to die is gain." What we may view as an earthly loss in Tyler's passing is the greatest representation of Christ's ultimate victory over death. Josh, Anni, and I went to visit him a few days after he left Purdue in the fall semester to enter hospice care. As we gathered to pray over Tyler, who seemed to be struggling to communicate that evening, he suddenly found his voice and began to pray over us: "Lord, I know those around me are struggling with things just as great as the burden of my cancer. Please provide someone in my absence who will listen to their story and point them back to you!"

Over the course of his second round of cancer, Tyler mentioned to me several times that he felt the need to redeem the time he had left on this earth by using his illness as a platform to share the gospel. This is what I respected the most about how Tyler lived his life over the past year. He didn't miss an opportunity to explain the strength, peace, and even joy he had in the midst of his battle with cancer because it came from a deep love for and faith in Jesus Christ.

I'm grateful for the lifetime of memories Tyler and I have shared—for the fun and laughter when we were together, the lessons he taught me, and the chance to see his many prayers answered. I'll always be thankful that God gave us so many fond memories and for the love I shared with my childhood friend.

When I went to visit him a week and a half ago, Tyler was having trouble staying awake. He was unable to say much of anything. But when he woke up after we had prayed for him, he said, "Amen," and then he strained to say one last thing to me: "One, four, three."

Tyler had a great affection for Mr. Rogers and embraced him as a role model in his life. "One, four, three" is a creative code Mr. Rogers used to count out the letters of "I love you," just as a creative God used Tyler to spread his "one, four, three" to a watching world. Love you, Tyler.

John Kruse came next, along with all of Tyler's college roommates.

Good evening. Unlike the past people you just saw, I've known Tyler a very, very short period of my life. Like most of those people who have come to know Tyler and his story this past year, I met Tyler through Purdue. After we had agreed to be freshman roommates through Facebook, I first met Tyler in Chicago for a Cubs game and dinner the night before.

After chatting online and meeting up in Chicago, we decided to be roommates for freshman year, and eventually even this year—along with the people who stand behind me. The decision to room with Tyler has affected me in so many ways that I couldn't have imagined—traveling to and from Marquette to watch basketball on a Wednesday night, going to California to see the Purdue bowl game, or being in the skybox for the win over Ohio State.

But for each of these great memories, Tyler had fights that went along with them. When we first met at dinner, he told me the story of the rod in his arm and how he had fought and battled through his first fight with cancer. Tyler told me about what got him through these hard times and how he came out stronger—his faith and his family.

He told me of his dreams of becoming a sportswriter, where he had traveled and still wanted to go, and of all the football games that were coming up that he wanted to be on the sidelines for. But God had other plans for Tyler. He chose Tyler to be a symbol of strength and faith in God's great plan. It was through his strength and faith in God's great plan that he was able to become the symbol of strength for not only a school, or a town, or a city, but an entire nation!

It's because of his strength and his story that people around the country are able to face their own afflictions with courage. So let's remember the strength that Tyler had, the strength that was derived from a pure faith, the love of his family, and the strong words of that Jimmy V speech: "Don't give up! Don't ever give up!"

Bigger than Sports

At this point in the service, the attention was turned to the screen, where many sports personalities paid tribute to Tyler via video messages.

Susan Brooks, U.S. Representative, Indiana Fifth Congressional District

Tyler Trent is a name known in households across the nation for his love of Purdue football and his inspiring passion and energy as a fan. Tyler always dreamed of becoming a Boilermaker and refused to allow cancer to get in his way. It is with that optimistic and positive outlook on life that Tyler inspired the nation. He's united Americans far and wide to be Boilermakers, and I hope we can all continue to be grateful and live every day as he did—Tyler Strong!

Ernie Johnson, *Turner Sports* Broadcaster, and Anchor of *NBA on TNT*

Tyler Trent. You talk about an impact player. All I can say is, thank you for reminding us to "rejoice always and pray continually and give thanks in all circumstances." And thanks for reminding me about the value of one day, one moment, one meeting—like we had on December 6.

It was life-changing, Christ-affirming, and it was so good for the soul. I'll never forget it.

Adrian Wojnarowski, ESPN Journalist and Columnist

To the Trent family: Tony, Kelly, Ethan, and Blake; to the Carmel/Indianapolis/Purdue communities. Tyler was such a reflection of your values, your strength, your determination—and while he cut a tremendous path of courage in life, there's no question that you all gave him the road map to do that. His legacy will live on, especially through the Trent family—and many of us hope you'll call upon us over time to help you do just that.

Tom Rinaldi, ESPN/ABC Sports Reporter and Broadcaster

When we walked into the Trent family's house this fall, we didn't really know fully what to expect. We knew what we were there to do—and that was to tell a story. What we had no idea about was how much the family's story and Tyler's courage and bravery would touch and ultimately change us—all of us—who were in that house that day.

Even more, we had no idea how far his courage, determination, spirit, and will would reach across the country and touch its collective hearts and—hopefully—touch its collective soul. That's exactly what Tyler would have wanted.

Sometimes we confuse "record" and "legacy." A *record* is what you've done; a *legacy* is what you've changed in the doing. Tyler's legacy is really just beginning, and his imprint upon all of us, I know, will probably never fade.

Scott Van Pelt, ESPN Anchor of *SportsCenter*

This is where I was sitting [in his ESPN studio] when I looked up on the wall [on a screen] at my co-host in his bedroom in Indiana, and I saw the light in his eyes, and I saw the smile. I was nervous, and Tyler Trent made me feel at ease. My co-host made me feel at ease! What an honor it was for us on our show to play a role in helping him make—as he told me—a dream come true. I've been so blessed to be at this for a long time. What have I ever done, what will I ever do, that is more meaningful than making Tyler's dream come true? Not a thing.

I was sitting right here last Tuesday when the news was shared with me that he had gone home to heaven, and that impacted us greatly as well—because we were so honored to play a small role in sharing his story, and his story impacted all of us in such a significant way.

That night on the show, I said we had saved a seat for him here, because we had. But I appreciate you all sharing a seat for me so I could be with you on this day, to celebrate his life—a life we are so honored intersected with ours.

Chris Ballard, General Manager of the Indianapolis Colts

I was drawn to him initially because of his story, but I kept going back because of his heart and his mind. To be honest with you, I never felt sorry for him because he just wouldn't allow it! His faith was so strong, and along the way, it strengthened mine! I was so humbled and honored to be around Tyler.

I couldn't stop coming back and found myself wanting more from a young man who had so much faith in God, so much love for his family and friends, so much forgiveness in his heart—so much passion for life, so much inner will and mental toughness that no matter the circumstances, he was gonna make a difference and change the world.

He made me a better person and gave me another perspective on life—and I'm thankful for it.

Family for Life

Tyler's family on the Crull side came to the stage together. Mike Crull, Tyler's uncle, was the first to speak.

As uncles and aunts—and a grandmother—we were blessed to share a special relationship with Tyler. Early on in Tyler's life, and particularly the weeks following news of his cancer diagnosis, we noticed something special emerging in our nephew, in our grandson. That something was his will and determination to use his life for good and for others—and most importantly, to glorify God. An example of that was his friendship and his advocacy for other cancer patients and medical research.

Tyler understood that at an early age, real difference-makers look far beyond themselves in their human condition, sick or otherwise. Although Tyler had a purpose and plan for every day (just ask his mother and father), Tyler's focus extended far beyond his physical life. His words, his actions, his spirit, his eyes all pointed to knowing Christ personally—and the homecoming with God that awaited him.

We are also blessed to see our children—Tyler's cousins—living out their lives with that same Christ-centered purpose and determination. Tyler's influence runs deep within them. God has been gracious and kind to our family. Tyler's life and legacy have been forever placed as the next building-blocks upon which God will continue to build and use the Trent/Crull/Campbell families. How wonderful God is to give us such meaning and purpose in life and in death!

Tyler had a special way of making everyone feel comfortable and at ease with his cancer, even in moments of intense pain and suffering. His ability to do that showed genuine—*genuine*—thoughtfulness and love. At times, it even resulted in some smiles and some laughter. One of those moments happened on Christmas day, just a few days ago, when we gathered together as a family.

We had all arrived, and as we began to visit, Tyler wanted everyone's attention before he moved from the wheelchair to the recliner. Only as Tyler would do, he wanted to remind us that when his parents would move him from the wheelchair to the recliner, there would be cries. He was having a little bit of fun with us but was being serious at the same time. Once he got comfortable in the recliner, he said with a slight grin, "I told you so! I told you so!" How thoughtful, how caring, how loving for him to think of us!

In every aspect of Tyler's life, he maintained an infectiously positive attitude and would often be heard—when asked, "How're you doing?" Tyler's response was, "Can't complain. Can't complain." This characterizes Tyler's life, his selfless determination to love, serve, and cheer for others. His family, friends, church, his medical team, his university, and the sports community knew this firsthand and up close.

Many of us know the "why" behind his focus: it was the gospel, the Good News of Jesus Christ. Like Jesus, Tyler's focus was on your life, on your soul, and on your relationship with God, who wants to know you for all eternity. These words of Jesus remind us of Tyler: "If anyone would come after me, let him deny himself and take up the cross and follow me . . . Whoever would save his life will lose it, but whoever loses his life for my sake will find it. For what will it profit a man if he gains the whole world but forfeits his soul?" (Matthew 16:24–26, ESV).

Mom, you've played a special role in caring for Tyler, as well as Kelly and Tony, Blake, and Ethan. And I've heard you say on many occasions, what an honor it has been to serve and to care for them. Mom, I can tell you that they are grateful for your care and for you loving them so well. Like Tyler, you have been a blessing and inspiration to our entire family and this community.

Tony, Kelly, Blake, and Ethan: we love you, we ache for you, but we know you are in the loving hands of God now and forever. Be assured you have the love and support of your family, including your church and the community represented here today and elsewhere. Thank you for sharing Tyler with all of us. His life has touched all of us so very deeply. You raised and cared for Tyler so well, and you sacrificed so much to help his hopes and his dreams come true.

May we all have a heart for God and someday hear the words that Tyler had already heard from his heavenly father: "Well done, Tyler! You've been a good and faithful servant. You have been faithful with a few things; I will put you in charge of much. Come and share in your master's happiness!"

Next to speak was Aaron Crull, Tyler's cousin.

First of all, thank you all for being here tonight. I think the support that our family has felt over the many years—especially the past few months—has been overwhelming, but in the best possible way.

I have the honor of speaking on behalf of a group of people that's very special to me. We vary in age from seven all the way up to twenty-seven. There are so many things that make us different and unique, but one thing we all have in common is that we've had the privilege of calling Tyler our cousin.

Now, I know that title may not mean very much to some, but for our family, it's profound! In our family, a cousin is a friend whom you are assigned at birth—sometimes for better or worse. It's different than a normal friendship because we know that, no matter what, we will always be family, and that means we will always be friends.

There's no better feeling for us than when we get all the cousins together in the same room. There's just so much laughter and so much joy—and so much energy and history in that group—and sometimes chaos! But right now, as we all gather and stand here together in this room, this group is feeling a gap. And it's not just that feeling that something is different or something's missing; it's that *someone* is missing—someone who's central to making us "us." We miss our cousin.

I think everyone will agree with me when I say you can't

replace Tyler Trent. He is absolutely one of a kind. I asked all my cousins to share one word that they would use to describe Tyler, and here's what they came up with: driven, witty, smart, selfless, compassionate, leader, magnetic, steadfast, brave, faithful, loyal, wise, honest, a fighter, devoted, strong—and inspiring. There are a lot of cousins.

Something we want you to understand is that we are not just describing how Tyler walked through his battle with cancer; we're describing who Tyler is. We've been blessed with a front-row seat to Tyler's whole life, and we can tell you with confidence that everything we listed above was true of Tyler before he was diagnosed with osteosarcoma and before he became the Purdue super-fan. All of these qualities were just simply amplified as he courageously entered that fight.

One of the qualities that became very apparent early on was that Tyler is smart—like, so smart. I would say that he went beyond "smart" and entered that "sharp" category. We all know that person who's just razor-sharp. And it's exactly how Tyler always has been. Like Trey alluded to, if you were in some kind of debate or disagreement, Tyler was the person you wanted on your side. And if Tyler wasn't on your side, it was probably a very short debate— and you were wrong.

God blessed Tyler with a brilliant mind, and he used that mind—that gift—to point others to the one who gave him that gift. When Tyler started his battle with cancer and walked through it with such grace, dignity, and faith, we were all inspired. And when he was given a national— and even global—stage, and he used it to raise money for research and uplift other people and glorify God, we were in awe.

But something we want you to understand is that when we watched how our cousin faced some of the greatest challenges a person can face in life, there's one thing that we were not. We were never surprised. Because the way that Tyler crushed and embarrassed cancer was just Tyler being Tyler. Tyler was driven, witty, smart, selfless, compassionate, a leader, magnetic, steadfast, brave, faithful, loyal, wise, honest, a fighter, devoted, strong—and inspiring—long before he was diagnosed with cancer, because that is who Tyler is.

And what we want you to know more than anything is that Tyler lived the incredible life that he lived not because of his love for his sports or his love for Purdue, or even his love for us—his family. Tyler lived with such purpose and drive because of his love for his creator and his dedication to Jesus Christ. And if you want to honor Tyler's life, or live like Tyler lived, get to know the God who created you and loves you more than you could ever know! That is what made Tyler, Tyler.

One last thing I want to say really quick: I just want to talk directly to Blake and Ethan. Guys, we are your cousins. Just like we are proud to call Tyler our cousin, we are proud to call you, Blake—and you, Ethan—our cousin. We are here for you; you are not going to walk through this alone because we're not going to let you! We love you, and we are here for you, and that will never, ever change!

A Brother's Love

Among the many speakers at the event was Tyler's youngest brother, Ethan. Surrounded by the support of his many cousins and his older brother, Blake, he courageously addressed the nearly two thousand people in attendance, struggling to get through the tears but ultimately reflecting the heart and spirit of Christ reflected in Tyler's life.

> I love Tyler. He was my role model, my best friend, and most importantly, my brother. Tonight, I'd like to share with you why I think my brother's life was worth celebrating.
>
> Personally, God made my brother in a very special way. Tyler was selfless. He had a story to tell, but he was more interested in hearing everyone else's stories. Tyler was very

positive and caring. I always remember that whenever I was feeling down about myself, Tyler would encourage me and tell me how special God made me. He would share with me verses like Psalm 118:24: "This is the day that the Lord has made . . . rejoice and be glad in it." I'll never forget how special God made my brother.

Second, Tyler is worth celebrating because of who he was to others. Tyler was loved by so many because he loved so many so well. Because Tyler was so selfless—so hopeful, and such a leader—even when he had cancer and was going through a hard time, he formed Teens with a Cause to serve others who had cancer—and their families—to make sure their needs were met. Tyler helped me learn how to interact with others and how to serve other people.

Finally, even though all these things are good, the reason I celebrate my brother the most is the way he served his purpose and how he lived his life. A verse that reminds me of Tyler is 1 Corinthians 10:31: "So whether you eat, drink, or whatever you do, do it all for the glory of God." Tyler lived for God, and even though I selfishly want him to be here on this earth with my family, all my cousins, and everyone we love, I can happily say he is in heaven with God and my Grandpa.

Tyler would want you to share his purpose for living. Tyler would want you to live your life for Jesus so he can see you soon in heaven. For tonight and years to come, I hope you can celebrate Tyler's life with me because of how special God made him—and how he lived his life. Thank you.

That Smile . . . Is No Accident

Others shared their remembrances of Tyler throughout the evening, and then Tyler's youth pastor and senior pastor, Joe Wittmer and Mark Vroegop, concluded the night with thoughts about Tyler and the savior whose grace sustained him through his suffering. These are the thoughts that Joe shared.

People who have known Tyler for any amount knew his smile. It was so much so that it became his nickname as a kid. They called him "Smiley." It was the first words that were spoken by Tom Rinaldi and his College Game Day tribute to Tyler the week before the Ohio State game: Tom said, "The smile!" The first day I met Tyler in 2012, he was smiling. The day before his death as I sat next to his bed holding his hand and joked, he smiled.

I was Tyler's youth pastor, occasional confidant, and friend. I knew him before the cancer as a boy who loved Jesus—a fierce board-game competitor, a leader, a servant, an occasional knucklehead, a person who loved figuring out the latest tech gadgets, and a kid who loved to goof around.

I knew him—before the cancer—to be smart, caring, fun, fierce, and always asking questions. When he messed up, he owned it—and if he did wrong, he tried to make it right. Before the cancer, he smiled—a lot. I knew Tyler during the cancer; I drove Tyler to chemo treatments during the first battle with cancer and talked with him about his fears, his hopes, his dreams, and his faith.

I shaved my head with Tyler and a group of leaders and students from our youth group when he started losing his hair. And he still smiled! I was at the hospital when the second round of cancer came, and we played board games together. We'd share favorite passages of scripture, we'd talk about the future, we'd pray—and he'd smile.

I visited Tyler at Purdue, walked the campus with him, saw his absolutely destroyed college dorm room, and held doors while he crutched through. I listened faithfully to his and Jake Heinzman's ridiculous podcast titled *Completely Unrelated*—with episode titles like "The Variability of Badgers" and "So Long, and Thanks for All the Fish!" And I heard his smile.

I wasn't there when he was diagnosed the third time, but I was there in the hospital again when he came home from Purdue, as sick as I'd ever seen him, yet every once in a while—a smile. I've been in the Trent home more times than I can imagine over the past months.

And as a lifelong Ohio State fan, I cheered when they lost to Purdue, and I saw that smile—as big as ever—on my screen at home. We talked, just weeks ago, about death and heaven and meeting Christ. I shared a song with Tyler titled "It Is Not Death to Die" and received a text the next day that said, "Dude! I love this song! I already listened to it twenty times!"—with a smiley emoji.

And, again, on December 31, as I walked out the door of his home, he mumbled feebly a good-bye, with a still-indomitable spirit—and a faint smile. That was his spirit: indomitable. That was the smile, always sincere and at the ready, that I believe won over a football team, a university, a sports world, and then a nation.

Here's the thing: I think everyone understands a good, Jesus-loving, smiling teen who's smart, funny, engaging, and cancer-free. The thing that is so unbelievable is a smile from someone who fought cancer again and again and again—who smiled when he told his story, but smiled even more when he heard yours.

I think the question that everyone—that a nation— is asking is, "How does that happen? How do you smile through suffering?" I want to submit to you that only a person who loves Jesus—and is loved by him—has this ability. Tyler is going to say in just a minute—because he's going to speak at his own memorial service in typical Tyler style—"If you don't believe in Christ, that strength is not possible!"

Tyler often spoke publicly about his faith, but listen, his faith was not just a nebulous belief in "something higher." His belief was that God sent his son, Jesus, to live a perfect life on this earth so that he could pay the price for imperfect people's sins through his death on the cross.

This death, Jesus' death, satisfied God's judgment on sin so that everyone who puts their hope and faith—Tyler's kind of faith—in Christ alone will be saved—not simply to a *future* hope of eternity in heaven, but a *present* hope that changes how we live, how we love others, and how we face suffering. This was a recurring theme and chorus for Tyler and me to review.

We would go through hope-filled verses found in the Bible that speak to suffering, verses like James 1:2–4 (NIV): "Consider it pure joy, my brothers and sisters, whenever you face trials of many kinds, because you know that the testing of your faith produces perseverance. Let perseverance finish its work so that you may be mature and complete, not lacking anything."

How does a person have joy in trials? Knowing the Good News—the gospel—that God is doing a work even in the suffering, even in the hardship. It is no coincidence that Tyler was known as mature beyond his years by so many; he had suffered so much! And God had used this to mature him so that Tyler might represent God well, showing off God and his glory through the story of Tyler's life we know so well.

That is why, again, you will hear Tyler quote one of his favorite verses and say, "God calls us to give thanks in all circumstances, not just the good circumstances." Another verse, Romans 5:3–5 (ESV), says, "Not only that, but we rejoice in our sufferings, knowing that suffering produces endurance, and endurance produces character, and character produces hope, and hope does not put us to shame, because God's love has been poured into our hearts through the Holy Spirit who has been given to us."

So how does a person keep smiling through cancer and in the face of death? Through a boast in a purpose, a mission, and a life that goes beyond themselves that reflects who God is in them. They do not simply smile; they glory in suffering because of the perseverance, the character, and the hope that will not be put to shame!

How many times over the past month have national icons spoken of Tyler's character, his perseverance, and his hope? These remarks are because Tyler was marked by a

God as one of his own—chosen and elevated to share his life with the world. Yes, so that others might fight cancer, but even more so that they might see Jesus through this young man—through Tyler Trent.

Some of my favorite verses that I went to the most when I was with Tyler—the ones I wrote on his hospital door on October 8, 2014—were 2 Corinthians 4:16–18 (NIV): "Therefore we do not lose heart. Though outwardly we are wasting away, yet inwardly we are being renewed day by day. For our light and momentary troubles are achieving for us an eternal glory that far outweighs them all. So we fix our eyes not on what is seen, but on what is unseen, for what is seen is temporary, but what is unseen is eternal."

See, Tyler would have really bad days! He would have moments of doubt, but ultimately, Tyler never lost heart. Again, so many people have been speaking to the heart of this young man—the tenacious, never-ending heart he had. This came from knowing that these troubles were achieving glory.

From a focus not on just what was seen but on what was eternal, Tyler's never-ending smile was caused by a never-ending hope in a never-failing God! Just a few verses earlier from my favorites in 2 Corinthians, we see God giving us a picture of Tyler's life. Listen to this: "But we have this treasure [which is the gospel, or the Good News, of Christ] in jars of clay [which are our mortal bodies] to show that this all-surpassing power is from God and not from us. We are hard pressed on every side, but not crushed; perplexed, but not in despair; persecuted, but not abandoned; struck down, but not destroyed. We always carry around in our body the death of Jesus, so that the life of Jesus may also be revealed in our body. For we who are alive are always being given over to death for Jesus' sake, so that his life may also be revealed in our mortal body. So then, death is at work in us, but life is at work in you" (2 Corinthians 4:7–12, NIV).

I truly believe this is what kept Tyler's smile, heart,

hope, and joy alive. When he was hard-pressed, perplexed, persecuted, and struck down by cancer, he continued to carry the hope of the gospel so that he was never crushed, never in total despair, never abandoned, never destroyed; so that the life of Christ was revealed in him; so that this life might be at work in you!

Tyler's life was so much more than cancer; Tyler's life was so much more than just his smile. Tyler's life was precious because it was connected to Christ. Tyler's hope, confidence, and security were rooted in Christ, and he wanted people to know that.

Before and after he was diagnosed with cancer, Tyler took time to pray and read the Bible. A saying he picked up from his dad was, "If you don't have time, make time." We don't know how many days we have left; no one here does. Only one person does: God. Tyler's life was a testimony to the power that God can have in and through a person.

So yes, I knew Tyler before the cancer. I knew Tyler during the cancer. But the thing I celebrate today is that I know Tyler after the cancer! I know Tyler is pain-free. I know he is wheelchair free and free from all the hardship that this life brings. I know that he is not only celebrating how God showed his glory through his life, but he is celebrating—in glory—God himself.

Tyler's grandfather died almost exactly a year ago. He died of cancer and had a huge impact on Tyler's battle. A quote Tyler carried with him from his grandfather was: "If I live or if I die, I win!" That win, again, was because of the truth of the gospel—the truth from God found in his Word and lived through those who love him. It's the truth known to us through his son, Jesus.

Tonight, as we celebrate the life of my friend Tyler Trent—as we remember his heart and his smile—please don't miss the power behind that smile and the message that mouth was looking to convey. And as I remember that message, we can do again what we did with Tyler many, many times—we can smile!

The final speaker to take the stage was Mark Vroegop, the Trents' pastor and friend.

You've heard a lot about Tyler already. His family has asked me to bring this service to a close with just a few thoughts about Tyler's primary message. The book of Ecclesiastes makes a very important statement; Solomon, one of the wisest men who ever walked the face of the earth, said, "It is better to go to the house of mourning than to go to the house of feasting, for this is the end of all mankind, and the living will lay it to heart" (Ecclesiastes 7:2, ESV).

What does that mean? It means something important happens in memorial services and in funerals and in celebration-of-life services. They invite us to stop and think. As a pastor, I've had the privilege of being a part of many, many—too many—memorial services. I must tell you, I come home from them, and I hug my wife longer. I tuck my kids in bed a little more gently. I savor moments. Why? Because the house of mourning is a really good teacher.

So you're here in this service for this twenty-year-old young man, and the questions that Tyler would want you to ask—the questions that I'm asking you to ask—are these: "What would we say at *your* funeral? What would be the impact of *your* life? What's the reason that you live? What kind of strength do you see in Tyler Trent?"

The house of mourning is meant to be a moment when we stop and go, "Hmm . . ." Tyler wanted you to ask these questions. We talked about this reality. A few weeks before he passed, I met with Tyler to ask about this very moment—this service—because I knew he would have very specific instructions as to what would happen.

We talked about the themes, the content of a message. It's a rare moment that a preacher says, "What do you want me to say? I'll say it, I'll say it!" Tyler wanted to be sure that he got this message out loud and clear, which was such a part of his soul and his aspirations—to be a sportswriter, to tell stories, and to get his message out.

This is even the reason why he had the vision for this book—so it could outlast him, even beyond this evening—for that message to continue to take flight.

Some of you are here because you've known Tyler most of his life, all of his life. Some of you, though, I'm guessing are here because you only knew Tyler as it relates to his cancer. And the question I want to think about is this: "That strength that Tyler possessed—what was the essence of it?"

You've heard it clearly so many times, so I'm not going to go in-depth because you've heard it. I just want to summarize. Tyler summarized it on a door in a hospital room in 2014 with four statements that came out of some things that we were talking about as a church: (1) God is holy, (2) I am not, (3) Jesus saves, and (4) Christ is my life. You can summarize the whole message of the Bible right there.

God is holy. He's the creator. He sets the rules. That's why you feel guilty when you do things that are wrong, because God sets the parameters. God is holy; I'm not. Tyler was a wonderfully valiant young man, but he wasn't perfect. He'd be the first to acknowledge that. He, like every human being, was a sinner. He knew it. He owned it. And the Bible tells us that the presence of sin in the world means something is broken. A funeral and osteosarcoma remind us of this—something isn't right!

We're going to end this service, and we're going to long for the day when this thing doesn't happen anymore. Death is a reminder that something is not right with the world. And cancer is just one little example; broken marriages, addictions, relationship conflicts, all sorts of personality issues, and conflicts with people are all reminders that something's not right with the world.

As beautiful as a sunrise or a sunset is, something's just not right. And the Bible tells us that it is the presence of sin, the brokenness we carry. We all have it. It's within all of us. We take it to every relationship. We take it to every job. We take it to everything we're involved in.

God's holy; I'm not—but Jesus saves. There's the turn! Tyler believed that two thousand years ago, Jesus came to pay the atonement for our sins, so that God could look at Tyler and count him forgiven—all because God took all of Jesus' righteousness and gave it to Tyler, and then took all of Tyler's sin and gave it to Jesus—and that's why Christians sing at funerals. Because we straight up believe that when God opens our books—or when he looks at Tyler's account—all he sees is "Paid in full by Jesus." When that gets hold of your soul and you know you've been granted forgiveness, it changes everything. It changes how you view money, how you view sexuality, how you view marriage, how you view work—and it also changes how you view cancer!

So before you is a young man who simply applied the central truth of the Bible to one aspect of his life: cancer. And I could show you person after person after person who are followers of Jesus who have done the exact same.

They may not be struggling with cancer, but they are struggling with a marriage that's really hard—and they're applying the gospel to it. They're struggling with a job that's disappointing—and they're applying the gospel to it. They're applying it to their singleness in which they are struggling to be hopeful, or to their infertility as a married couple. They're taking this gospel and bringing it into these areas. This funeral reminds us of this central message: if the gospel can transform a kid with osteosarcoma, it can transform anything.

God's holy; I'm not. Jesus saves. Christ is my life. That's what you saw in Tyler Trent. Colossians 3 says, "Set your minds on things that are above, not on things that are on the earth. For you . . . died, and your life is hidden with Christ in God" (vv. 2–3). This means when the message of forgiveness through Christ gets inside somebody, it gets inside everything, transforming everything from the inside out.

So what Tyler demonstrated was the transformative power not just of believing the gospel, but also of living in and through the gospel. That is why his death actually can create life in you. That is, in essence, what made Tyler strong. He had the hope that transformed everything about him.

But I must tell you, it's not only Tyler who possesses this strength. I've seen it in Tony, who had to tell his son—not once, not twice, but three times—that he had cancer. I've seen it in his mom, Kelly, who willingly shared her son with hundreds, even thousands, of people in the last days, weeks, and months of his life.

I've seen it in Blake and Ethan as they loved their brother while he was battling cancer, and I've seen it in other members of the Trent, Crull, and Campbell families. But I must tell you, even more broadly, as a pastor, I've seen this over and over and over. You got to see it in one young man because the spotlight of national media was shining on him, but I could take you to funeral after funeral after funeral and show you the same thing—because what was true about Tyler is also true of everyone who is a follower of Jesus when the gospel gets inside their souls.

Therefore, if you're here and you're a Christian, can I just remind you that this is what you signed up for? You signed up for "Christ is my life." My hope is that you'll use this instruction of Tyler's life, and you'll leave here and say, "You know what? Game on! I need to follow Jesus even more fully!"

If you're not yet a Christian, in the first century when Peter and John were hauled before a tribunal to be questioned, the most intelligent people in the city were grilling them. But their interrogators noticed something unusual about them and said, "These men are uneducated, but it just seems as though they've been with Jesus!"

When Stephen was being pelted with rocks, the crowds

looked and saw something about his face, and it looked like that of an angel. In the first century and throughout the history of the church, the watching world got to see what happens when gospel-loving, Jesus-centered people die or when they are falsely accused.

If I can just be really candid with you, this is one of the greatest examples that I could lay before you as a pastor of what it means to love Jesus. And if you're still that person who's kind of on the fence or trying to figure out what it means to be a follower of Jesus, could I just tell you that, for some reason, in God's providence, he has orchestrated the intersection of your life with Tyler Trent's. And I don't believe for a second that this is by accident.

I believe the reason he has done this is to show you what it means to be a Christ follower. Tyler's passion was not just to make it through osteosarcoma; his passion was to help people like you, and me, to have hope; and that's why 1 Thessalonians 5 is so incredibly powerful! "Rejoice always, pray without ceasing, give thanks in all circumstances . . ." And I want to end with this as a point of emphasis: ". . . for this is the will of God in Christ Jesus for you." For you, there's no rejoicing, there's no praying, there's no giving thanks without being "in" Christ Jesus. This means trusting him as your only hope, even as Tyler trusted him.

This was the essence of Tyler's life. It's also the essence of the gospel. It makes the difference for all of eternity, and it is one of the last things Tyler said to me: "Be sure they know, and be sure they have hope!"

One of the beautiful family traditions of the Trent family was that, on Sunday evenings, they would pray the Lord's Prayer together. We're going to invite you to do that. After we pray the Lord's Prayer together, there's going to be another sort of family tradition—a moment in which they'd like to invite you into their family.

Finally, Kelly would sing to all of her sons as she would tuck them into bed "You Are My Sunshine." You know that song? Please don't make me sing it, okay? And as the casket is rolled out, we're going to sing that song together, just like we're in their family room, in their bedroom tucking in their kids. They are so grateful that you've been a part of this experience—a part of their family.

Let's pray:

Oh, Father in heaven, we thank you that this is a moment for all of us to stop and pause and consider. We know that death is a reminder that something is wrong with the world, and we long for the day when death and tears and crime will be no more. But until that day, we pronounce over this casket and in this moment that this is not over! There's coming a day, Jesus, when you're going to return and the resurrection of the dead will take place—an empty tomb at Easter was the beginning of that moment. Jesus, you bought the right back then to make this moment right in the future. And so we lament, we mourn, and yet we trust and believe and hope in you.

And so, Lord, we pray—oh Lord, we pray—that there would be many, many who will come to faith in Christ, many who will look back and say, "It was at Tyler Trent's funeral when I realized I was a sinner, when I realized I needed a savior, and when I confessed my sins and chose to receive Christ." Lord, would many, many join the ranks of followers of Jesus who know this hope.

Oh Lord, we now ask for your help. This family needs your grace. It's been a long road, and we pray that you would still be with them, even as you've promised you would be every step of the way. And we thank you for the community of faith who helps us in these moments. We pray this in Jesus' name, amen.

Then everyone stood and sang "You Are My Sunshine" as Tyler's family members and closest friends rolled his casket out of the room.

Photo courtesy of Purdue University

On behalf of The Trent Family,
we would like to say thank you so much for helping us
upset cancer.

VISIT TYLERTRENTBOOK.COM
Learn more about Tyler and his goal of raising $1,000,000
for cancer research and families battling cancer.

FOLLOW US ON TWITTER
Tyler Trent - @theTylerTrent
Tony Trent - @TonyTrent10
Kelly Trent - @Kat9798

» Share a picture of you with your book on
Twitter, Facebook, and Instagram.

» Tag @theTylerTrent and tell us how this
book has inspired you.

» Use hashtags #TylerStrong and #TheUpset
to spread the word.

INVITE TONY AND KELLY TRENT TO SPEAK AT YOUR EVENT
For questions about speaking engagements or other
inquiries, please contact us at info@tylertrentbook.com

Real People. Real Stories.

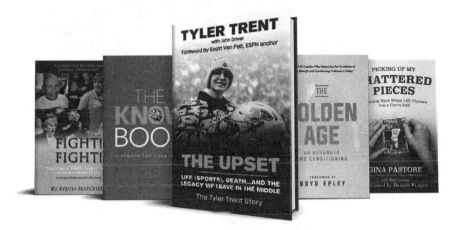

CORE™

You have a story that is worth sharing, a story that the world needs to hear. Let us help you! Learn more at www.thecoremediagroup.com.

For questions about books or other inquiries, please contact info@thecoremediagroup.com.

FOLLOW US

The Core Media Group, Inc.
@SpiritInStory